Hall of Best Knowledge.

HO

BK

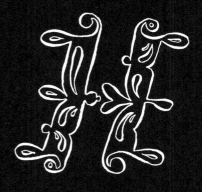

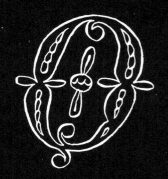

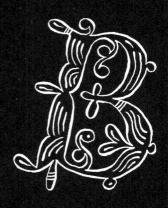

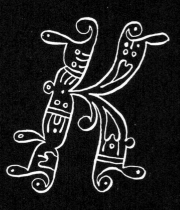

Fantagraphics Books
7563 Lake City Way NE
Seattle, Washington 98115

Published by Gary Groth & Kim Thompson
Edited by Gary Groth
Promotion by Eric Reynolds
Production and design assistance by Jacob Covey

To receive a full-color catalog of comics, graphic novels, prose novels,
and other fine works of artistry, call 1-800-657-1100,
or visit www.fantagraphics.com.
You may order books at our web site or by phone.

Distributed in the U.S. by W.W. Norton and Company, Inc.
(212-354-5000)

Distributed in Canada by Raincoast Books (800-663-5714)

Distributed in the United Kingdom by Turnaround Distribution
(108-829-3009)

ISBN: 978-1-56097-910-4

First Fantagraphics printing: April, 2008

Printed in China

❧ IDEAS, IN ORDER *of* APPEARANCE ❧

LEGACY.
Wherein both you and the author live forever.

KUDOS.
Wherein the author allows things to bristle with pure energy.

CONVERSATION.
Wherein the author declares war/victory.

SPIRITUALITY.
Wherein the author channels Socrates.

TOPIC NAME WITHHELD.
Wherein the author is sensitive to your needs.

UNEXPECTED EXAM.
Wherein the author journeys to the center of your mind.

EXAM RESULTS.
Wherein the author emerges from your mind covered in honey.

METAPHOR.
Wherein the author eschews chit-chat in favour of art.

DEATH.
Wherein the author introduces "offness."

CANCELLED II.
Wherein the author tests your dedication.

PONY.
Wherein the author does not saddle up.

SUPERSTITION.
Wherein the author can see hidden tears.

MINDWINDS.
Wherein the author saves Poetry.

GOD.
WHEREIN THE AUTHOR YAWNS.

HUMOUR.
Wherein the author pines for humour that takes away dignity.

CANCELLED IV.
Wherein the author is again denied recompense.

LISTENING.
Wherein the author mentions "so & so."

ORIGINALITY.
Wherein the author plays a haunting melody.

EPISTEMOLOGY.
Wherein the author knows, and you do not, and it is funny.

A SHORT ANNOUNCEMENT.
Wherein the author knows who you were talking about.

SPRING.
Wherein the author pulls you up off your knees.

cancelled V.
Wherein the author encourages epic singing.

SOLITUDE.
Wherein the author eats the sweetest of rose-soil berries.

UTOPIA.
WHEREIN THE AUTHOR DREAMS OF A RENAISSANCE FESTIVAL PLANET.

PARTY.
Wherein the author is denied.

WEALTH.
Wherein the author can't understand why you are poor.

ART.
Wherein the author holds an oily mirror up to nature.

a recent invention.
Wherein the author proudly reveals a... thing.

ELECTRICITY.
Wherein the author soars high above.

THE CALLIGRAPALS.
Wherein the author creates a comic work for the genteel.

MIND SAFARI.
Wherein the author plans an educational outing.

MIND SAFARI II.
Wherein the author ventures out into unknown wilderness.

BIRTHDAY.
Wherein the author consults mathematical knowledge.

ECCENTRICITY.
Wherein the author does not want to be ignored.

FAME.
Wherein the author introduces you to a glowing seed.

GOODBYE.
Wherein the author is not, at any point, crying.

SURELY, I JEST.
Wherein the author has you laugh and learn.

CANCELLED VI.
Wherein the author is too important to deal with you.

FENCING.
Wherein the author uses french words to great effect.

EXPRESSION.
WHEREIN THE AUTHOR DECODES.

ENTERTAINMENT.
Wherein the author dazzles you with foil.

CALLIGRAPALS II.
Wherein the author pens a delicate graphic poem.

PERFORMANCE EVALUATION.
Wherein the author objectively evaluates.

CANCELLED VII.
Wherein the author hates you.

JOY.
Wherein the author mentions airborne leeches.

CALLIGRAPALS III.
Wherein the author draws a short fiction.

CAMP.
Wherein... the author... cannot... breathe...

END.

Hall of Best Knowledge.

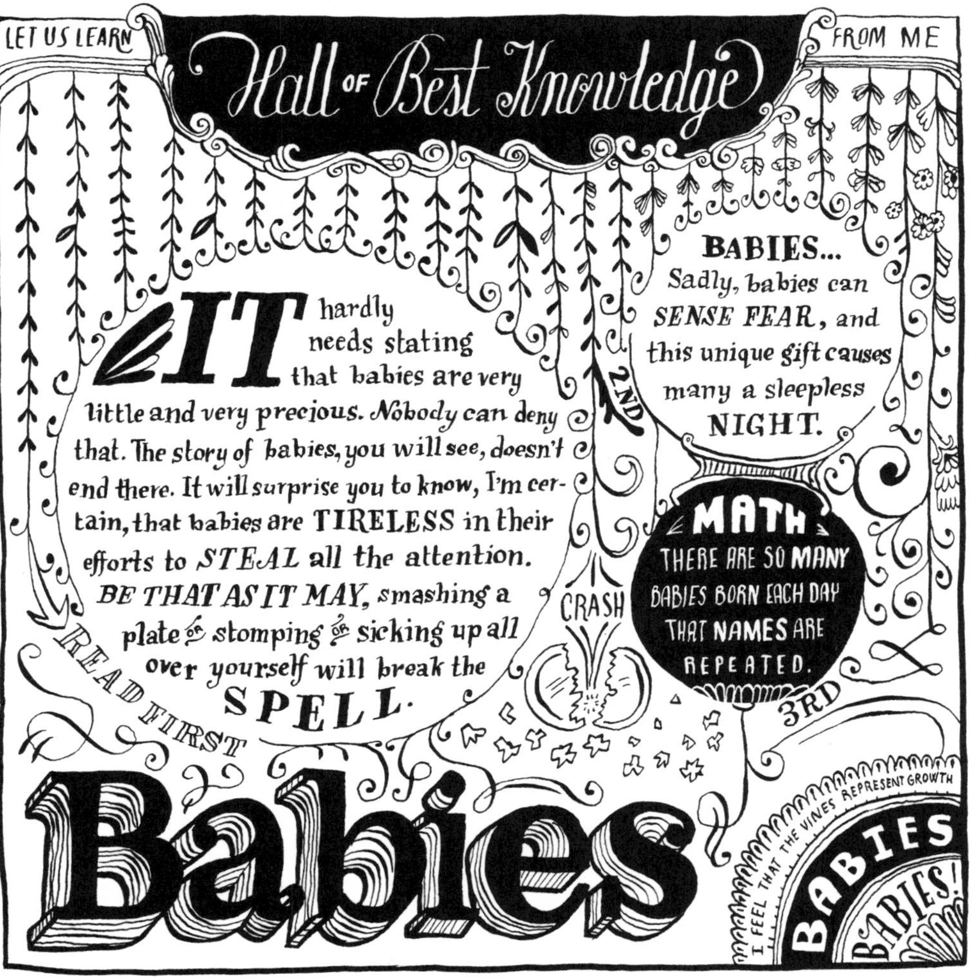

LET US LEARN
Hall of Best Knowledge
FROM ME
IT hardly needs stating that babies are very little and very precious. Nobody can deny that. The story of babies, you will see, doesn't end there. It will surprise you to know, I'm certain, that babies are TIRELESS in their efforts to STEAL all the attention. BE THAT AS IT MAY, smashing a plate or stomping or sicking up all over yourself will break the SPELL.
READ FIRST
2ND
BABIES... Sadly, babies can SENSE FEAR, and this unique gift causes many a sleepless NIGHT.
CRASH
MATH
THERE ARE SO MANY BABIES BORN EACH DAY THAT NAMES ARE REPEATED.
3RD
Babies
I FEEL THAT THE VINES REPRESENT GROWTH
BABIES
BABIES!
BABIES

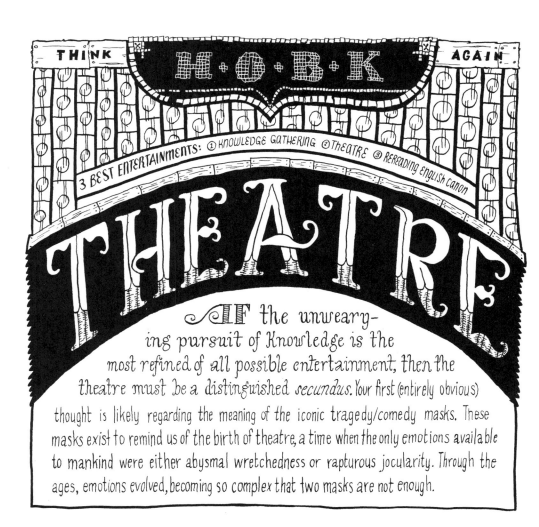

THINK · AGAIN

H·O·B·K

3 BEST ENTERTAINMENTS: ① KNOWLEDGE GATHERING ② THEATRE ③ REREADING ENGLISH CANON

THEATRE

IF the unweary-
ing pursuit of knowledge is the
most refined of all possible entertainment, then the
theatre must be a distinguished *secundus*. Your first (entirely obvious)
thought is likely regarding the meaning of the iconic tragedy/comedy masks. These
masks exist to remind us of the birth of theatre, a time when the only emotions available
to mankind were either abysmal wretchedness or rapturous jocularity. Through the
ages, emotions evolved, becoming so complex that two masks are not enough.

Hall of Best Knowledge

majestic   *insight*

It is the most common of knowledge that when given the chance to judge your own **BEAUTY** you do so, with a very desperate vigor. There are, it's clear, many fine venues for this kind of appraisal:

BEAUTY

reflective shop windows, magazines, even faces of close friends. Be that as it may, you are, sadly, wasting time better spent searching for the true judge of beauty: THE BEHOLDER. Upon looking into its single, intense eye, you will be judged authoritatively with one grunted word: Beautiful. Ugly.

CAREFUL THERE ARE THOSE AMONG US WHO FIND BEAUTY IN *EVERYTHING*, EVEN THE CRUSH AND STINK OF A SUBWAY! THESE PEOPLE ARE CARELESSLY BURNING UP ALL SENSITIVITY AND WILL ONE DAY BE UNABLE TO DETECT TRUE BEAUTY.

HOW DO I ACQUIRE THE KNOWLEDGE I SHARE WITH YOU? THE ANSWER IS @ MUCH SOLITARY THOUGHT @ RARE, ANCIENT SECRET LIBRARIES.

WHAT PERCENTAGE OF MY KNOWLEDGE HAVE I SHARED? IT IS, YOU WILL BE SURPRISED TO KNOW, TOO SMALL A PERCENTAGE TO NOTE.

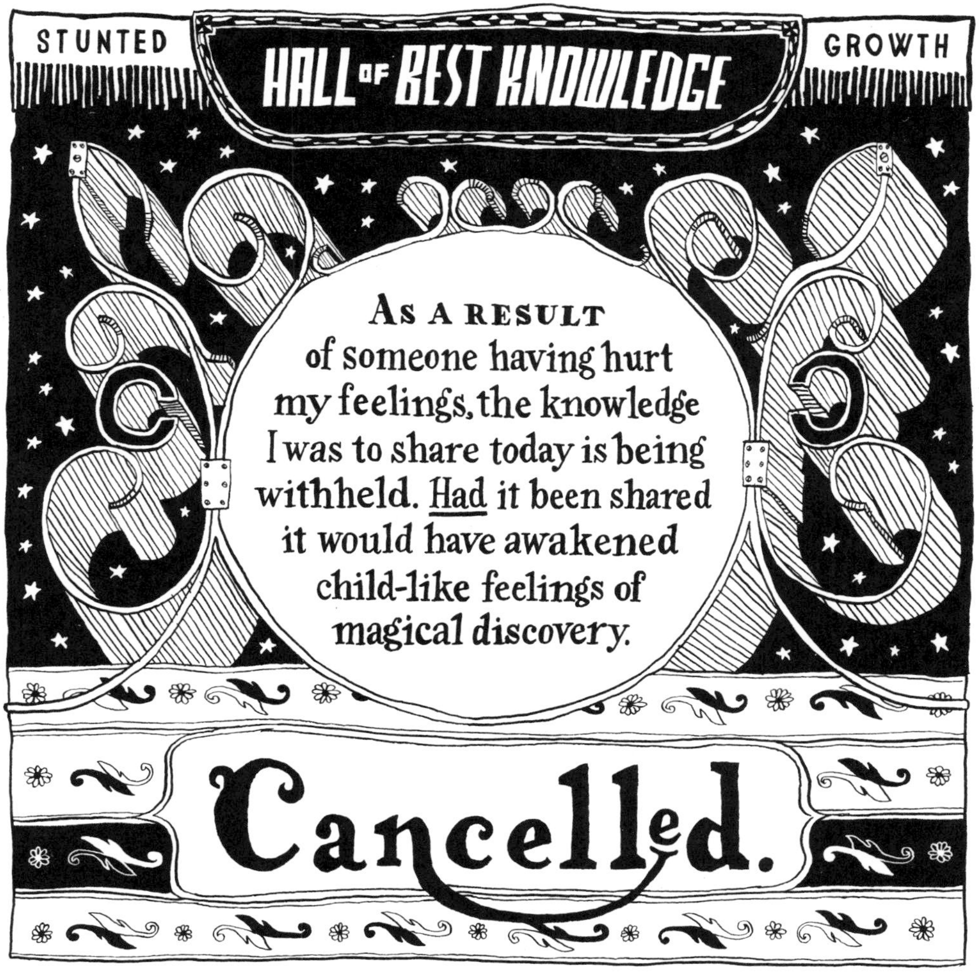
STUNTED
HALL OF BEST KNOWLEDGE
GROWTH
As a result of someone having hurt my feelings, the knowledge I was to share today is being withheld. Had it been shared it would have awakened child-like feelings of magical discovery.
Cancelled.

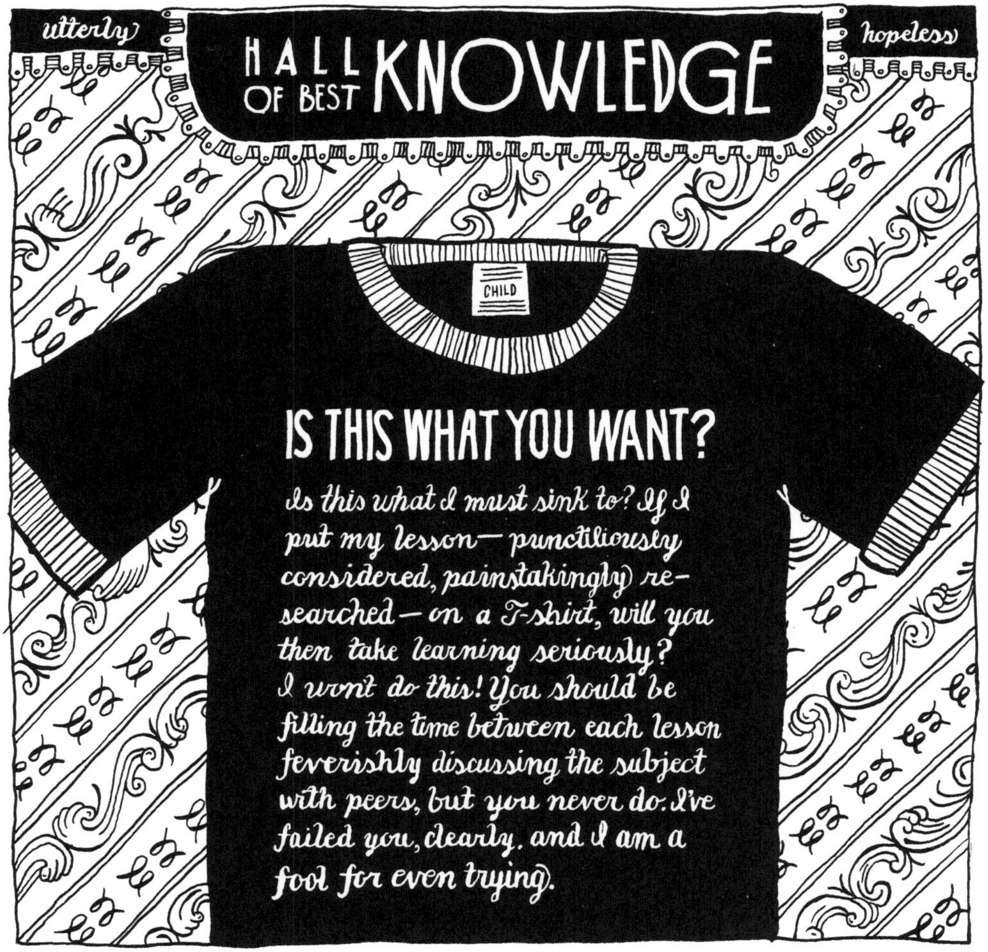

utterly
HALL OF BEST KNOWLEDGE
hopeless
CHILD
IS THIS WHAT YOU WANT?
Is this what I must sink to? If I put my lesson—punctiliously considered, painstakingly re-searched—on a T-shirt, will you then take learning seriously? I won't do this! You should be filling the time between each lesson feverishly discussing the subject with peers, but you never do. I've failed you, clearly, and I am a fool for even trying.

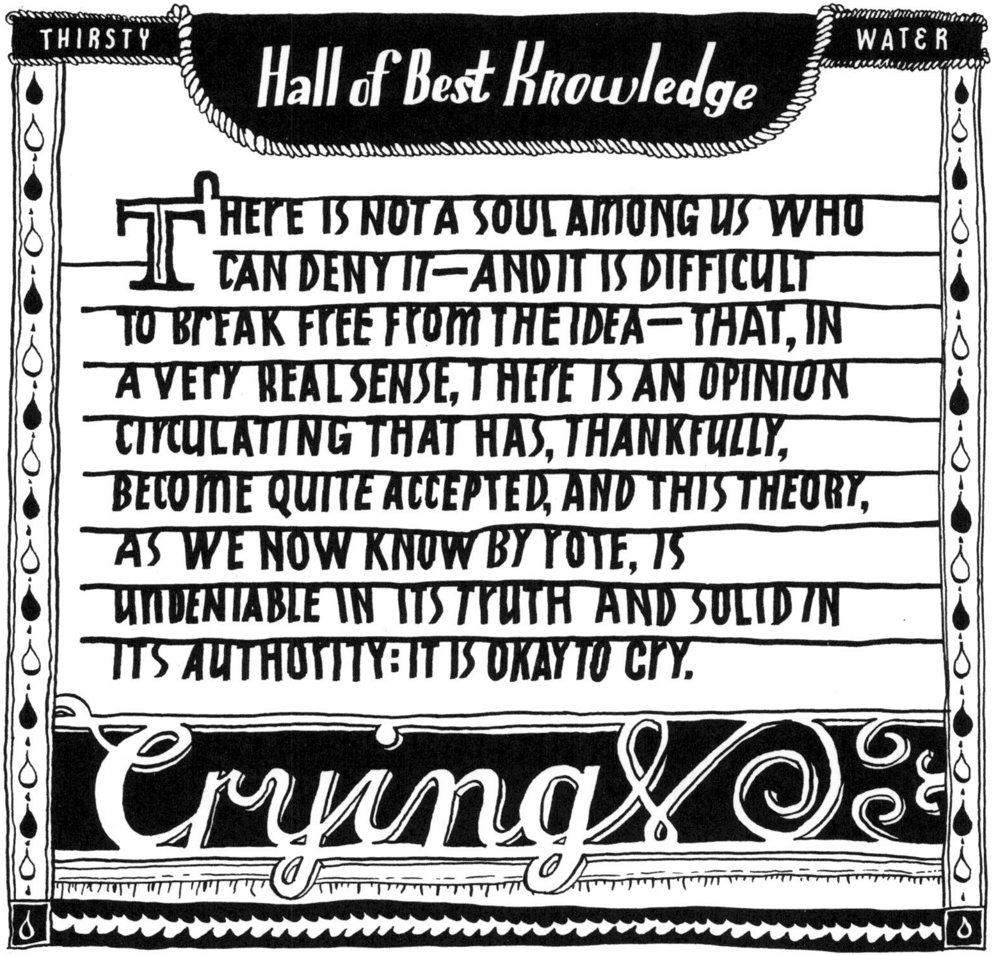
THIRSTY
Hall of Best Knowledge
WATER
THERE IS NOT A SOUL AMONG US WHO CAN DENY IT—AND IT IS DIFFICULT TO BREAK FREE FROM THE IDEA—THAT, IN A VERY REAL SENSE, THERE IS AN OPINION CIRCULATING THAT HAS, THANKFULLY, BECOME QUITE ACCEPTED, AND THIS THEORY, AS WE NOW KNOW BY VOTE, IS UNDENIABLE IN ITS TRUTH AND SOLID IN ITS AUTHORITY: IT IS OKAY TO CRY.
Crying &c

HALL OF BEST KNOWLEDGE

WISDOM

CAKE

There's no denying that, at this very moment, there exists on earth your exact replica; a perfect twin; a double. As you happily read what I have written here, he or she is living on the *Exact Opposite* side of the earth, doing the *Exact Opposite* of what you are currently doing, only *better* and *more successfully!* It's profoundly painful for

DOPPELGÄNGER

you, no doubt, to be told this. Firstly, it means that you'll never be able to meet your doppelgänger (*opposite location*) and secondly, because you are both *better* than each other there is a tragic paradox: you are both *FAILURES.*

WHEN YOU ARE
QUESTIONING YOUR WORTH
DANCING
LOUDLY REJOICING

YOUR DOUBLE IS
BEING TOASTED IN A FLATTERING WAY
PERFECTLY STILL, HANDSOMELY SO
ENCHANTINGLY, ACHINGLY MELANCHOLIC

IF YOU HAVE A TWIN BROTHER · LIKE I PERSONALLY DO · THEN YOU ARE FREE OF THE PARADOX
I AM NOT A FAILURE

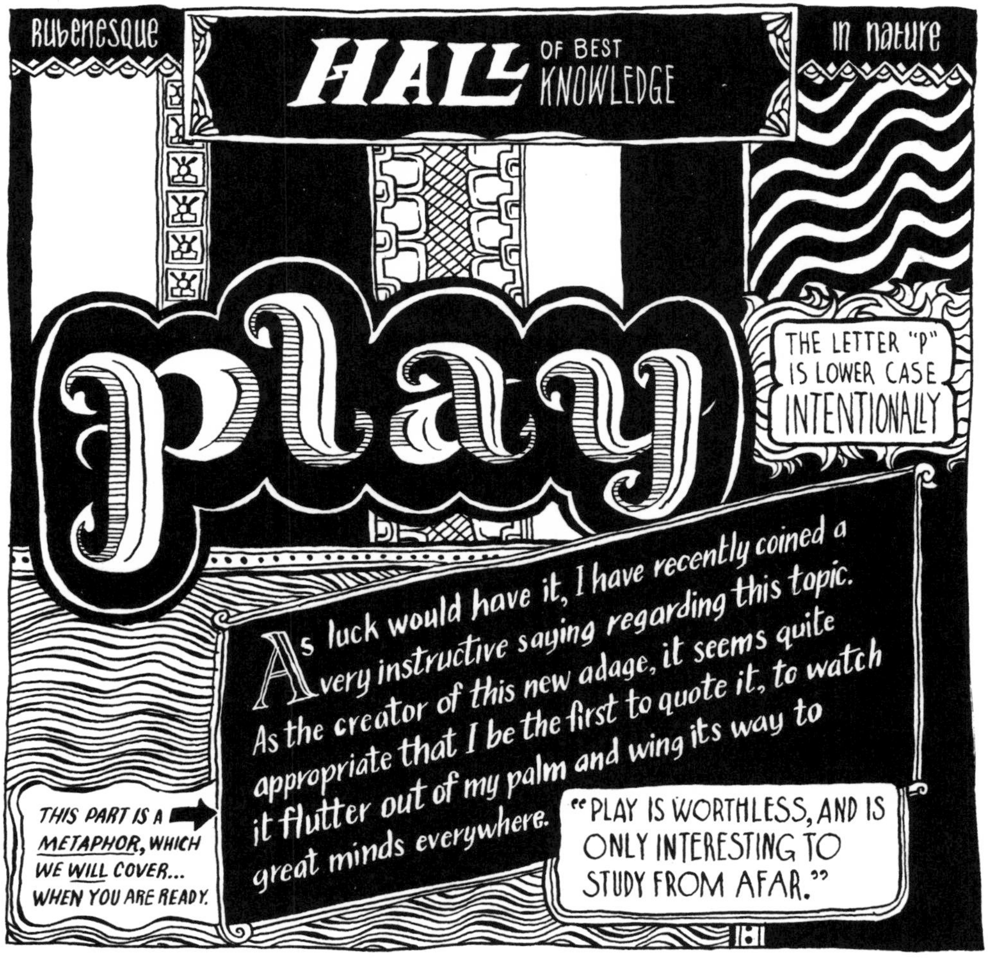
Rubenesque
HALL OF BEST KNOWLEDGE
in nature
play
THE LETTER "P" IS LOWER CASE INTENTIONALLY
As luck would have it, I have recently coined a very instructive saying regarding this topic. As the creator of this new adage, it seems quite appropriate that I be the first to quote it, to watch it flutter out of my palm and wing its way to great minds everywhere.
THIS PART IS A METAPHOR, WHICH WE WILL COVER... WHEN YOU ARE READY.
"PLAY IS WORTHLESS, AND IS ONLY INTERESTING TO STUDY FROM AFAR."

Hall of Best Knowledge

THOUGHT IN FLIGHT

STRANGERS

OF NOTE

Let's be frank and speak seriously about something irrefutably true: strangers are **not** friends you haven't met. To wit, it's true you haven't met them, but they cannot, you will soon agree, be called **FRIENDS**. Do **you** have **friends** who wait silently with you at the bus stop and stare? Or don't stare, not even **ONCE?** Making you feel undesirable? You need not answer.

THIS TOO!

STRANGERS ARE UNABLE THERE ARE, IN A VERY REAL IT WOULD SEEM, TO WAY, AT LEAST 30 STRANGERS MAKE INTERESTING IN EACH AND EVERY CITY. CONVERSATION.

FREQUENCY
OF STRANGERS STARING

| NOW | NOT NOW | NOW | NOW |

HALL OF BEST KNOWLEDGE

Simply put, legacy is the ghost of your genius haunting the world after your death with your life's collected wisdom. Legacy is created when you have a baby, when a bronze statue is made in your honour or when you write an autobiography. So! You must make as many babies as possible, erect statues on every corner and watch tables crumble under the weight of your life story. If none of that is feasible, you must make a "mental" baby in the minds of all who meet you, building "mental" statues in their skulls and surrounding their brain with the pages of your "mental" autobiography. When you pass on, these people become your legacy, possessed by your shrieking thoughts.

LEGACY

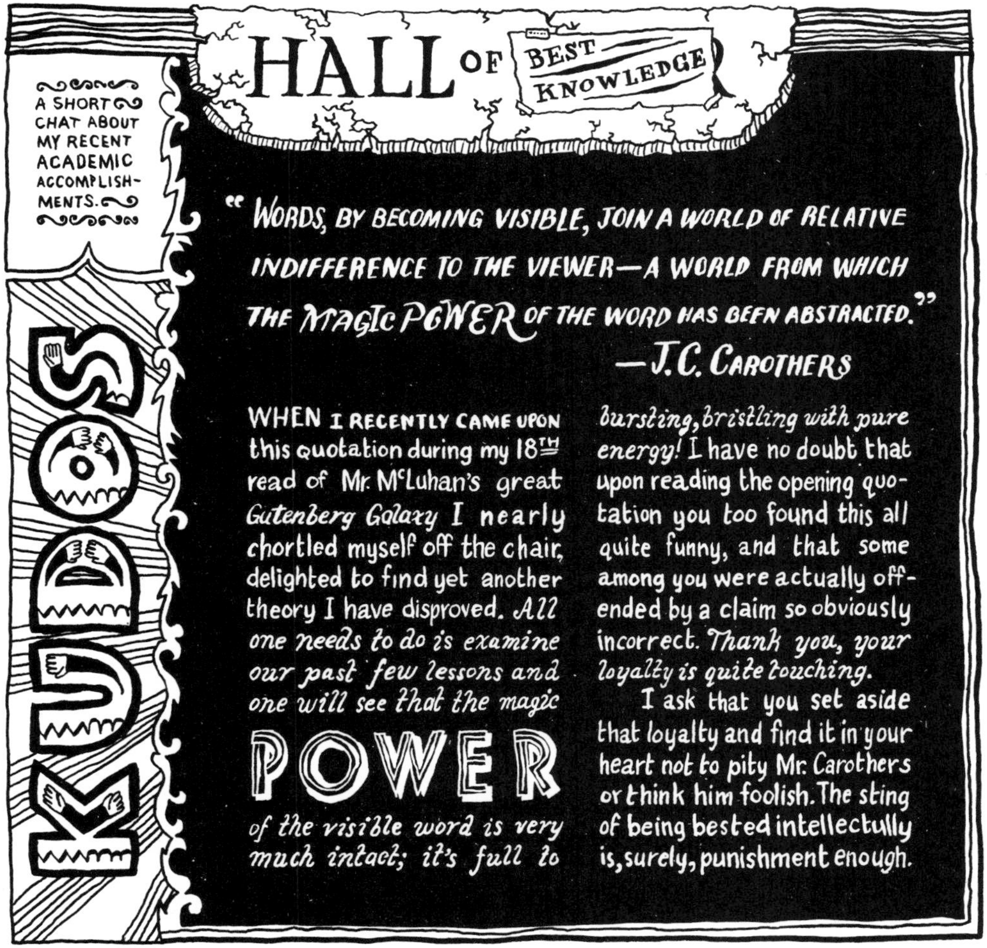
HALL OF BEST KNOWLEDGE
A SHORT CHAT ABOUT MY RECENT ACADEMIC ACCOMPLISHMENTS.
KUDOS
"WORDS, BY BECOMING VISIBLE, JOIN A WORLD OF RELATIVE INDIFFERENCE TO THE VIEWER—A WORLD FROM WHICH THE MAGIC POWER OF THE WORD HAS BEEN ABSTRACTED."
—J.C. CAROTHERS
WHEN I RECENTLY CAME UPON this quotation during my 18th read of Mr. McLuhan's great *Gutenberg Galaxy* I nearly chortled myself off the chair, delighted to find yet another theory I have disproved. *All one needs to do is examine our past few lessons and one will see that the magic* POWER *of the visible word is very much intact; it's full to bursting, bristling with pure energy!* I have no doubt that upon reading the opening quotation you too found this all quite funny, and that some among you were actually offended by a claim so obviously incorrect. *Thank you, your loyalty is quite touching.*
I ask that you set aside that loyalty and find it in your heart not to pity Mr. Carothers or think him foolish. The sting of being bested intellectully is, surely, punishment enough.

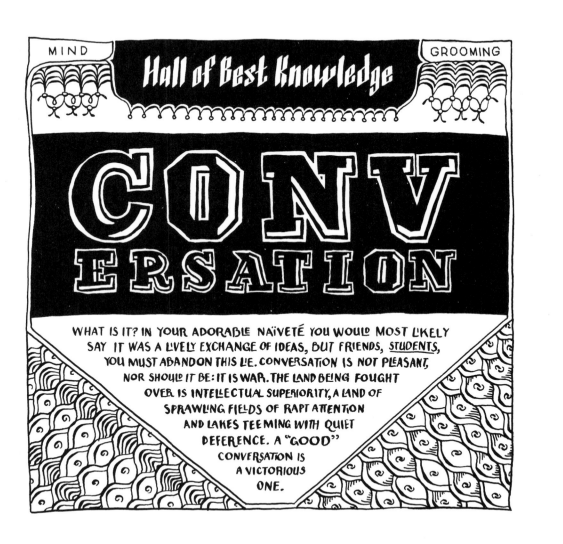

Hall of Best Knowledge

MIND

GROOMING

CONVERSATION

WHAT IS IT? IN YOUR ADORABLE NAÏVETÉ YOU WOULD MOST LIKELY SAY IT WAS A LIVELY EXCHANGE OF IDEAS, BUT FRIENDS, STUDENTS, YOU MUST ABANDON THIS LIE. CONVERSATION IS NOT PLEASANT, NOR SHOULD IT BE: IT IS WAR. THE LAND BEING FOUGHT OVER IS INTELLECTUAL SUPERIORITY, A LAND OF SPRAWLING FIELDS OF RAPT ATTENTION AND LAKES TEEMING WITH QUIET DEFERENCE. A "GOOD" CONVERSATION IS A VICTORIOUS ONE.

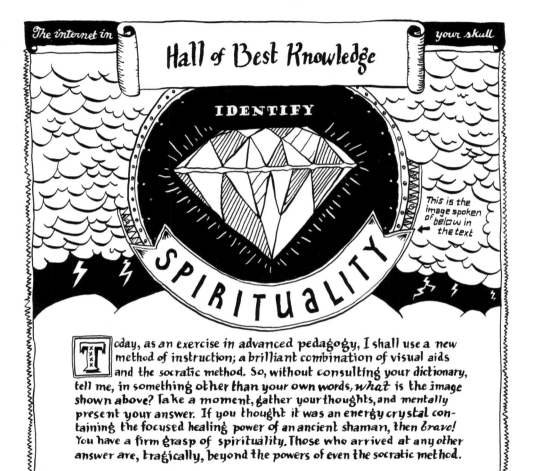

The internet in your skull
Hall of Best Knowledge
IDENTIFY
This is the image spoken of below in the text
SPIRITUALITY
Today, as an exercise in advanced pedagogy, I shall use a new method of instruction; a brilliant combination of visual aids and the socratic method. So, without consulting your dictionary, tell me, in something other than your own words, what is the image shown above? Take a moment, gather your thoughts, and mentally present your answer. If you thought it was an energy crystal containing the focused healing power of an ancient shaman, then bravo! You have a firm grasp of spirituality. Those who arrived at any other answer are, tragically, beyond the powers of even the socratic method.

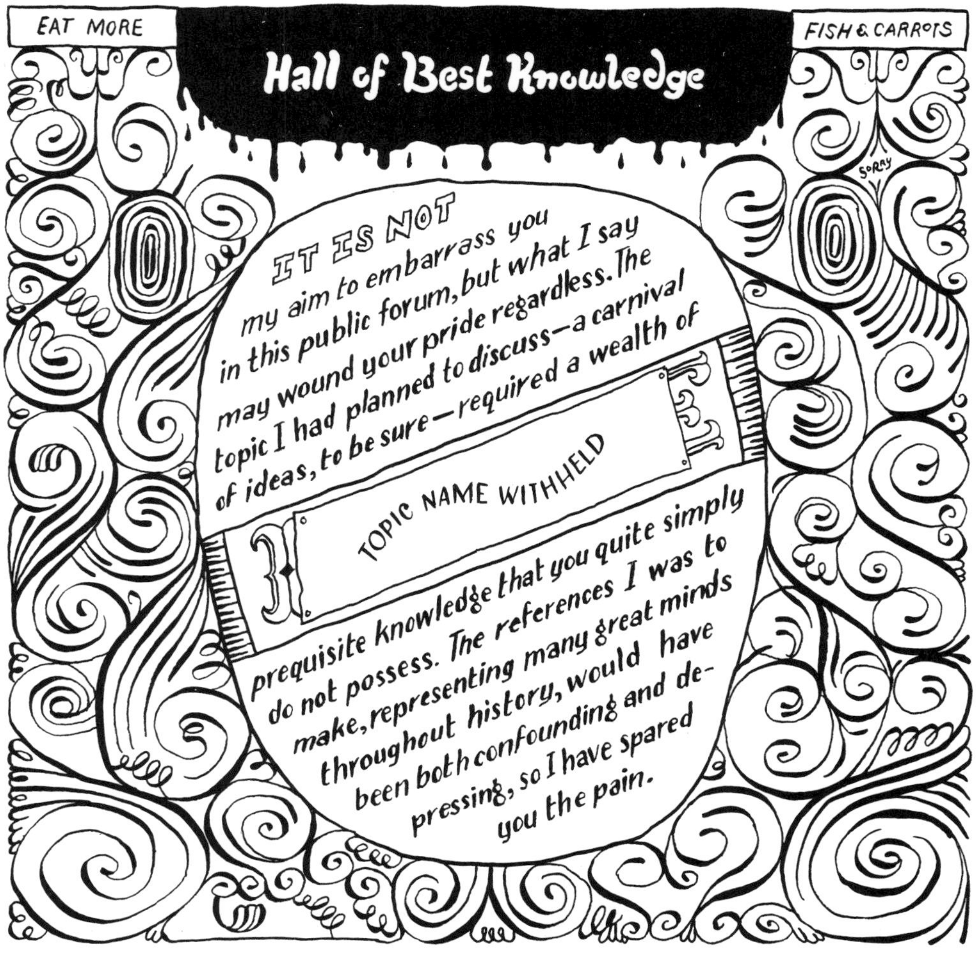

EAT MORE
Hall of Best Knowledge
FISH & CARROTS
SORRY
IT IS NOT my aim to embarrass you in this public forum, but what I say may wound your pride regardless. The topic I had planned to discuss—a carnival of ideas, to be sure—required a wealth of
TOPIC NAME WITHHELD
prequisite knowledge that you quite simply do not possess. The references I was to make, representing many great minds throughout history, would have been both confounding and depressing, so I have spared you the pain.

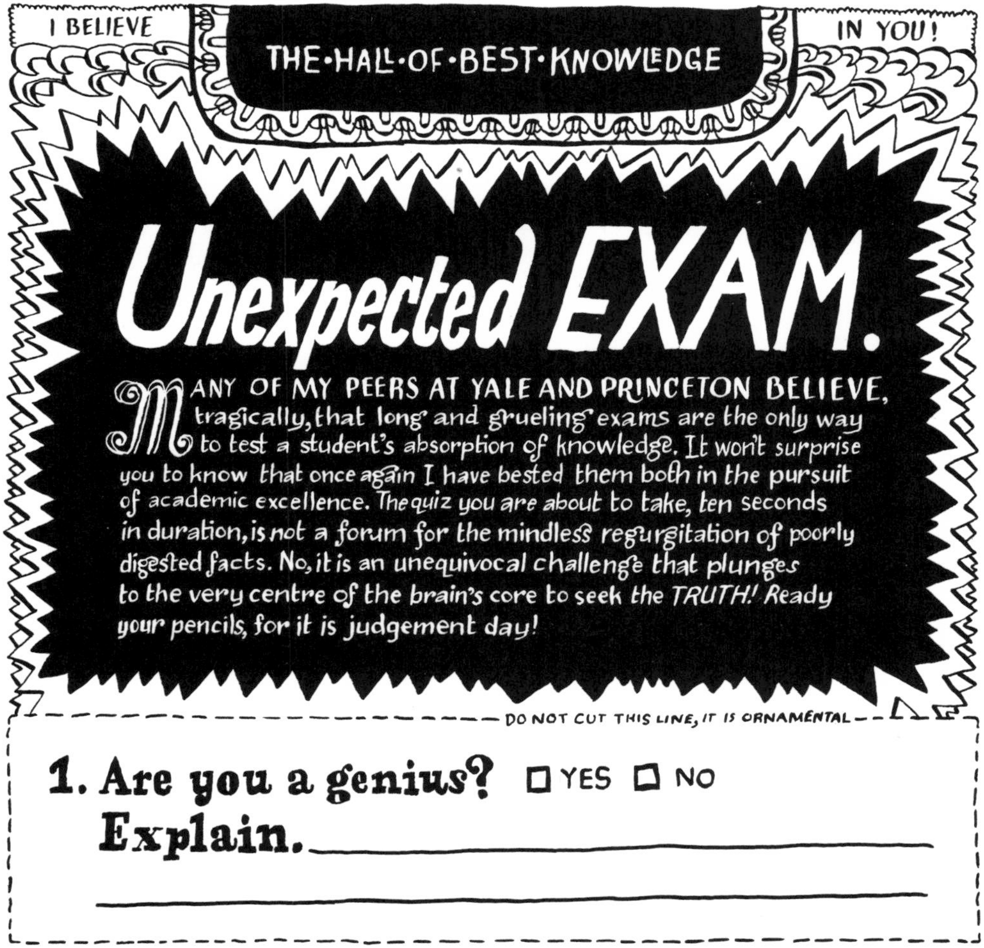
I BELIEVE
THE·HALL·OF·BEST·KNOWLEDGE
IN YOU!
Unexpected EXAM.
MANY OF MY PEERS AT YALE AND PRINCETON BELIEVE, tragically, that long and grueling exams are the only way to test a student's absorption of knowledge. It won't surprise you to know that once again I have bested them both in the pursuit of academic excellence. The quiz you are about to take, ten seconds in duration, is not a forum for the mindless regurgitation of poorly digested facts. No, it is an unequivocal challenge that plunges to the very centre of the brain's core to seek the TRUTH! Ready your pencils, for it is judgement day!
DO NOT CUT THIS LINE, IT IS ORNAMENTAL
1. Are you a genius? ☐ YES ☐ NO
Explain.

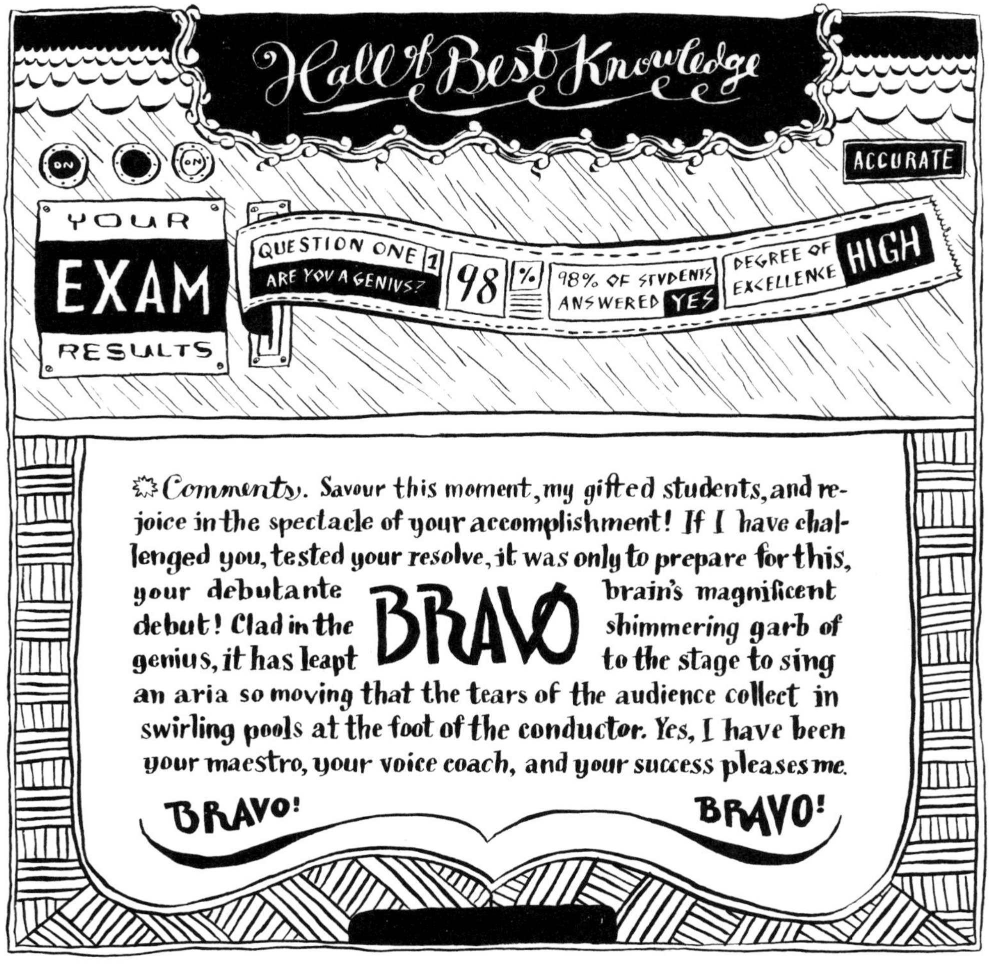
Hall of Best Knowledge
ON
ON
ACCURATE
YOUR
EXAM
RESULTS
QUESTION ONE 1
ARE YOU A GENIUS?
98
%
98% OF STUDENTS ANSWERED YES
DEGREE OF EXCELLENCE
HIGH
Comments. Savour this moment, my gifted students, and rejoice in the spectacle of your accomplishment! If I have challenged you, tested your resolve, it was only to prepare for this, your debutante brain's magnificent debut! Clad in the shimmering garb of genius, it has leapt to the stage to sing an aria so moving that the tears of the audience collect in swirling pools at the foot of the conductor. Yes, I have been your maestro, your voice coach, and your success pleases me.
BRAVO
BRAVO!
BRAVO!

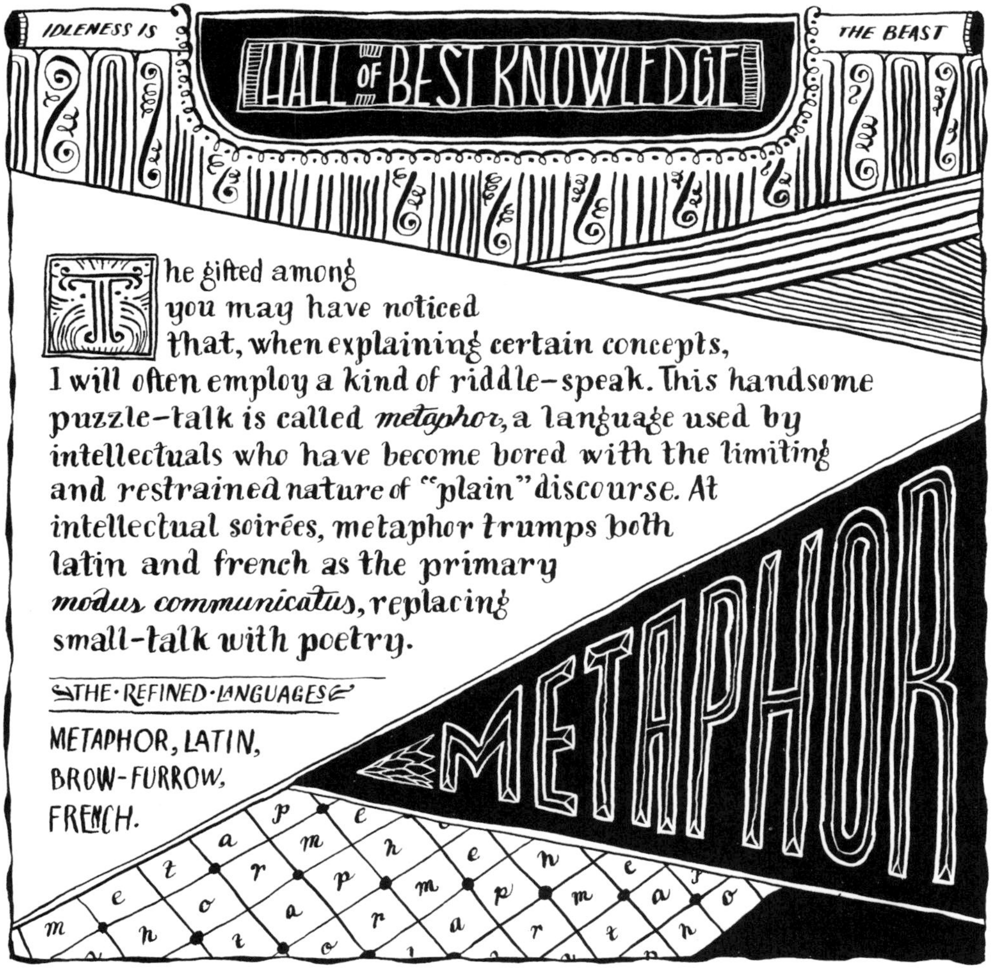
IDLENESS IS
HALL OF BEST KNOWLEDGE
THE BEAST
The gifted among you may have noticed that, when explaining certain concepts, I will often employ a kind of riddle-speak. This handsome puzzle-talk is called *metaphor*, a language used by intellectuals who have become bored with the limiting and restrained nature of "plain" discourse. At intellectual soirées, metaphor trumps both latin and french as the primary *modus communicatus*, replacing small-talk with poetry.
THE·REFINED·LANGUAGES
METAPHOR, LATIN, BROW-FURROW, FRENCH.
METAPHOR

HALL OF BEST KNOWLEDGE

Death

IT GOES WITHOUT SAYING THAT MANY fine philosophers have been driven mad trying to understand this concept. Had they simply asked *ME, I* could HAVE set them at ease! Alas, for them it is too late, but not for you. **DEATH**, my students, it is not a destination. It is a destined state of OFFNESS. The machine, its energy depleted, switches off, and we do not wonder where it has gone because we see it, right there in front of us, in a state of offness. So love your machines & ponies now, for in OFFNESS they cannot respond.

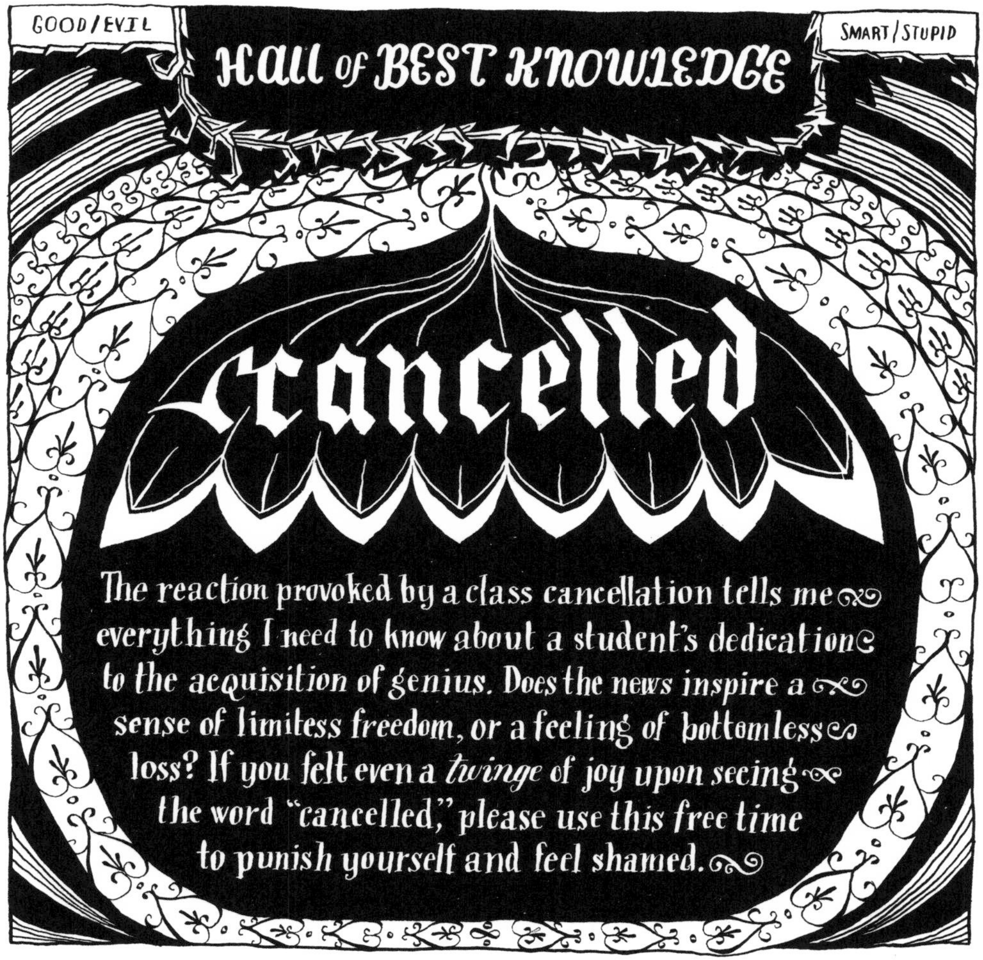
GOOD / EVIL
HALL of BEST KNOWLEDGE
SMART / STUPID
cancelled
The reaction provoked by a class cancellation tells me everything I need to know about a student's dedication to the acquisition of genius. Does the news inspire a sense of limitless freedom, or a feeling of bottomless loss? If you felt even a *twinge* of joy upon seeing the word "cancelled," please use this free time to punish yourself and feel shamed.

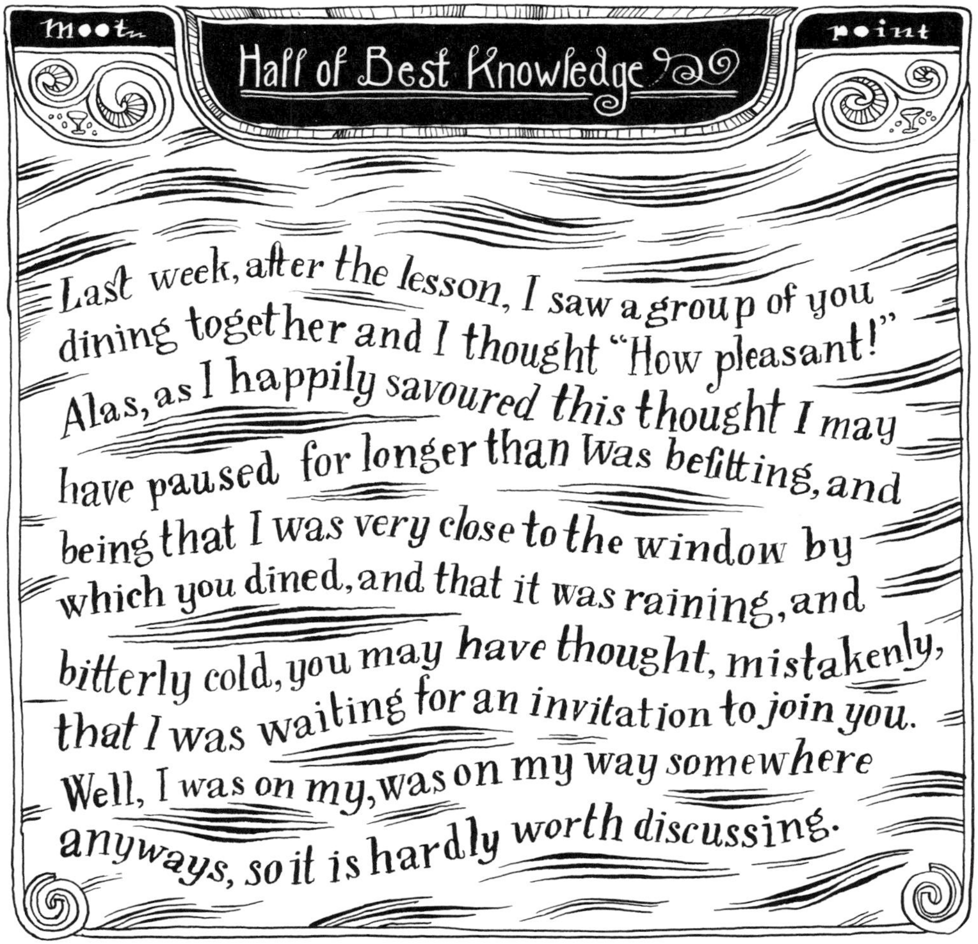
moot
point
Hall of Best Knowledge
Last week, after the lesson, I saw a group of you dining together and I thought "How pleasant!" Alas, as I happily savoured this thought I may have paused for longer than was befitting, and being that I was very close to the window by which you dined, and that it was raining, and bitterly cold, you may have thought, mistakenly, that I was waiting for an invitation to join you. Well, I was on my, was on my way somewhere anyways, so it is hardly worth discussing.

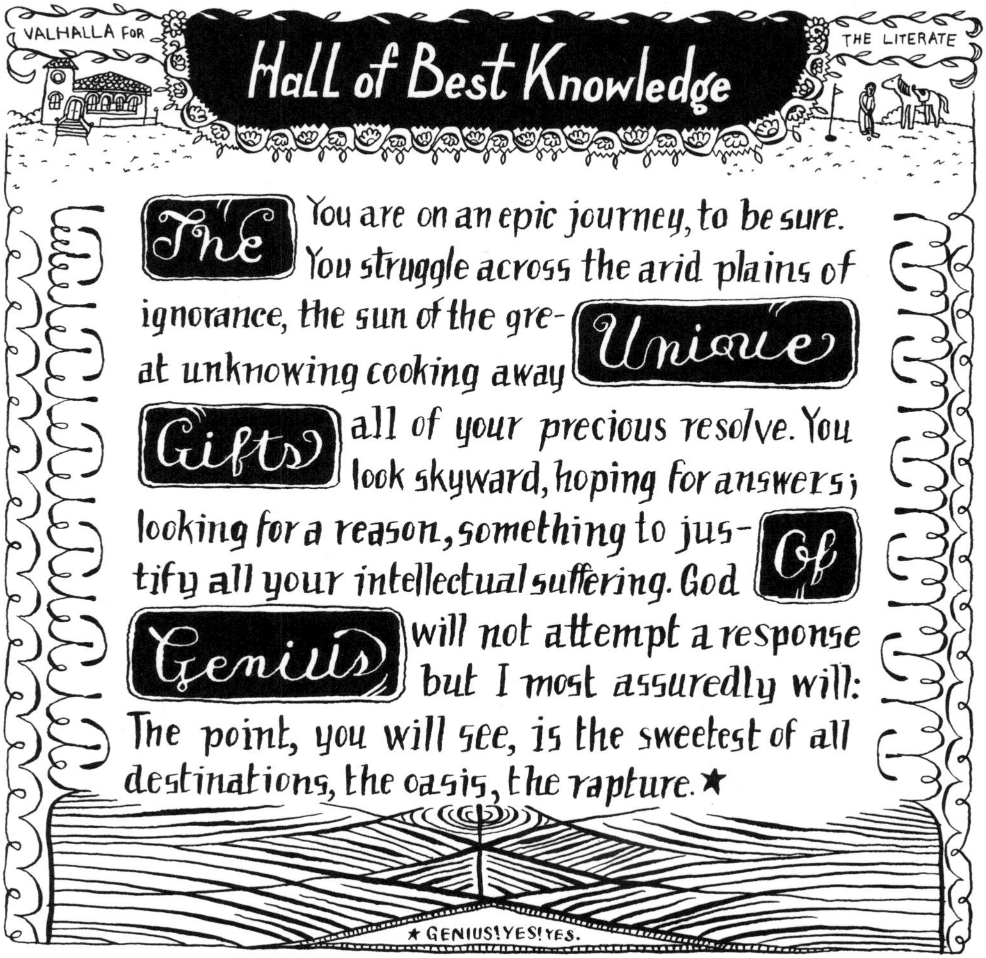
VALHALLA FOR
Hall of Best Knowledge
THE LITERATE
The Unique Gifts Of Genius
You are on an epic journey, to be sure. You struggle across the arid plains of ignorance, the sun of the great unknowing cooking away all of your precious resolve. You look skyward, hoping for answers; looking for a reason, something to justify all your intellectual suffering. God will not attempt a response but I most assuredly will: The point, you will see, is the sweetest of all destinations, the oasis, the rapture. ★
★ GENIUS! YES! YES.

BRAIN CONTROLS
THE ALL OF YOU
Hall of Best Knowledge
WITHOUT GENIUS
WITH GENIUS
Constant fatigue, or threat of fatigue.
Body invigorated by increased brain energy!
Crying.
Brain forbids waste of important eye fluids!
Bruises, cuts, scrapes.
Accidents are prevented by careful logic!
Odour.
Powerful computer brain issues reminders to address hygiene!
Not kissing anyone, ever.
Constant, complicated kissing
Weak, pedestrian tastebuds.
All but the finest wines taste like foul juice from compost!
Fingers of an ogre mash piano keys.
Shouts of "bravo"!
World looks flat, two dimensional.
Colours you can smell!
PHYSICAL
GIFTS of GENIUS

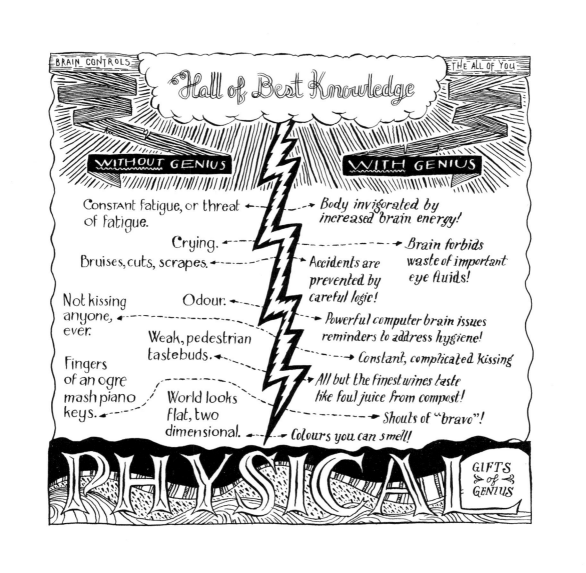

INFLAMMATION OF THE THOUGHT

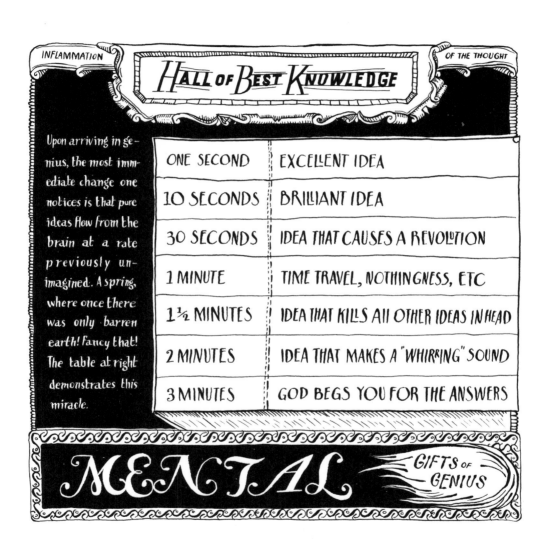

HALL OF BEST KNOWLEDGE

Upon arriving in genius, the most immediate change one notices is that pure ideas flow from the brain at a rate previously unimagined. A spring, where once there was only barren earth! Fancy that! The table at right demonstrates this miracle.

ONE SECOND	EXCELLENT IDEA
10 SECONDS	BRILLIANT IDEA
30 SECONDS	IDEA THAT CAUSES A REVOLUTION
1 MINUTE	TIME TRAVEL, NOTHINGNESS, ETC
1½ MINUTES	IDEA THAT KILLS ALL OTHER IDEAS IN HEAD
2 MINUTES	IDEA THAT MAKES A "WHIRRING" SOUND
3 MINUTES	GOD BEGS YOU FOR THE ANSWERS

MENTAL

GIFTS OF GENIUS

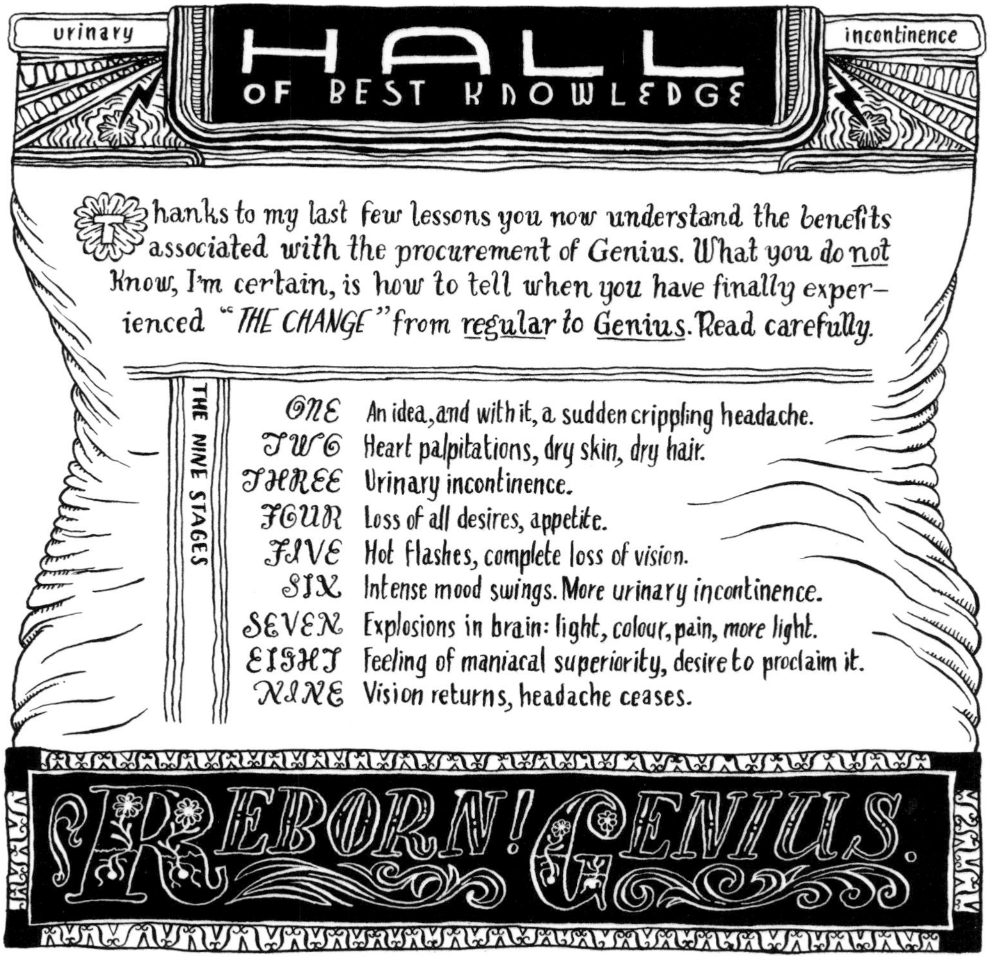
urinary
HALL
OF BEST KNOWLEDGE
incontinence
Thanks to my last few lessons you now understand the benefits associated with the procurement of Genius. What you do not know, I'm certain, is how to tell when you have finally experienced "THE CHANGE" from regular to Genius. Read carefully.
THE NINE STAGES
ONE An idea, and with it, a sudden crippling headache.
TWO Heart palpitations, dry skin, dry hair.
THREE Urinary incontinence.
FOUR Loss of all desires, appetite.
FIVE Hot flashes, complete loss of vision.
SIX Intense mood swings. More urinary incontinence.
SEVEN Explosions in brain: light, colour, pain, more light.
EIGHT Feeling of maniacal superiority, desire to proclaim it.
NINE Vision returns, headache ceases.
REBORN! GENIUS.

VIBRANT BRAINS ON PARADE

HALL OF BEST KNOWLEDGE

LIBRARY

It goes without saying that in the primitive ages of man, one's worth was directly linked to one's MUSCULAR STRENGTH, and if one could savagely bludgeon a food source while grunting happily then one was surely the talk of the cave. Happily, times have changed and now it is our PERSONAL LIBRARIES — not our muscles — that truly show our worth. When a guest views your library, the effect should be akin to the speechless awe inspired by the primitive hunter tearing off his animal skin to display glistening, sustenance-providing muscles. If the viewer is not left trembling before your impressive selection of books, then there is work to be done!

Dear Santa,

Let it be known, sir, that I only write this letter to satisfy Mother, who has threatened to confiscate my OED should I not comply.

I assume you know what I will ask for, as I have asked for it every year, but perhaps you misunderstood last year's request. Both Mother and Brother suggested that the reason for this might have been that I employed too many "grown up" words, and that you might find this distasteful. While I find the idea of dumbing down this letter insulting to both of us, I shall try it only because the ends justify the means. Ahem.

Santa, I WOULD LIKE PLEASE ~~WANT~~ TO BE THE SMARTEST PERSON IN THE WORLD, ALSO KNOWN AS A GENIUS. SANTA, I READ REALLY LONG BOOKS ALL DAY AND ALSO ALL NIGHT, SANTA. SANTA, I READ LOTS AND I GET HEADACHES THAT MAKE ME WANT TO CRY BUT I DON'T CRY AND INSTEAD, I READ MORE, SANTA. SANTA, I KNOW THAT SMART PEOPLE ARE NEVER SAD, AND NO ~~FEW~~ HEADACHES, AND ALSO THEY ARE WELL LIKED. ~~NOBODY~~ SANTA. PLEASE? PLEASE. THANK YOU.

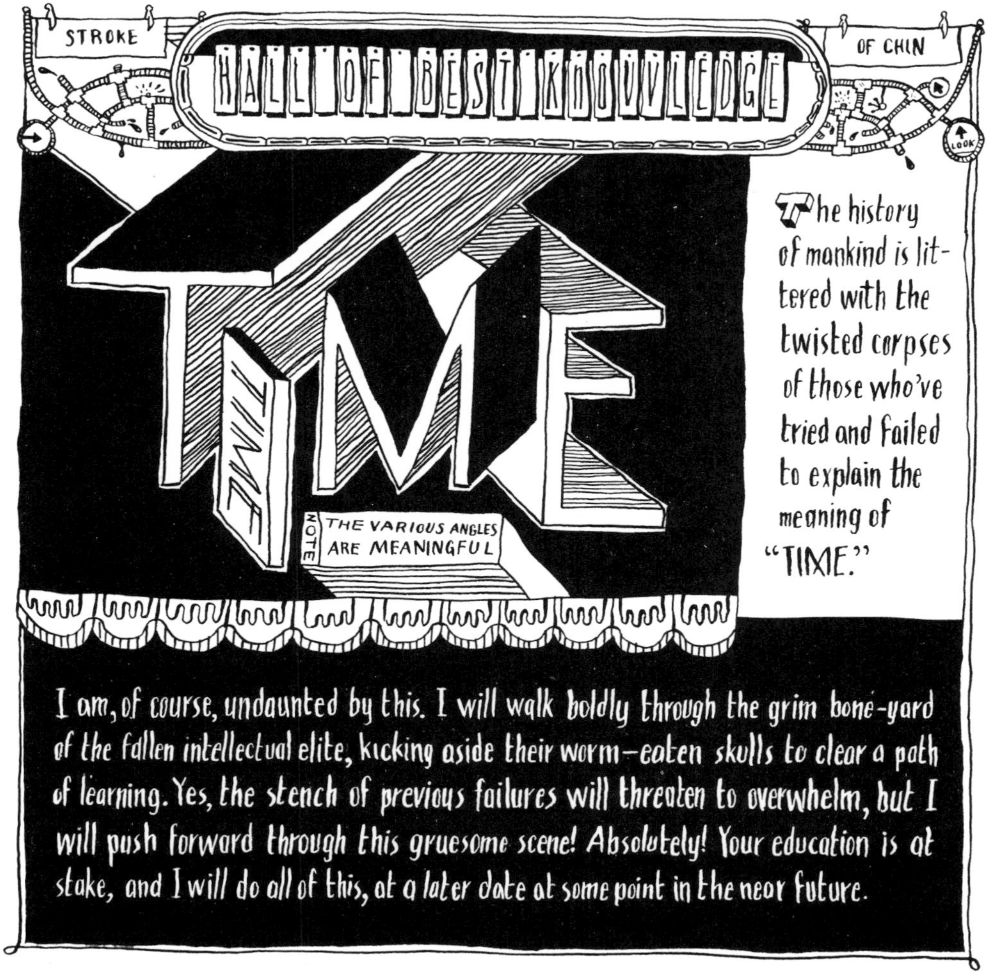
STROKE
HALL OF BEST KNOWLEDGE
OF CHIN
LOOK
TIME
TIME
NOTE
THE VARIOUS ANGLES ARE MEANINGFUL
The history of mankind is littered with the twisted corpses of those who've tried and failed to explain the meaning of "TIME."
I am, of course, undaunted by this. I will walk boldly through the grim bone-yard of the fallen intellectual elite, kicking aside their worm-eaten skulls to clear a path of learning. Yes, the stench of previous failures will threaten to overwhelm, but I will push forward through this gruesome scene! Absolutely! Your education is at stake, and I will do all of this, at a later date at some point in the near future.

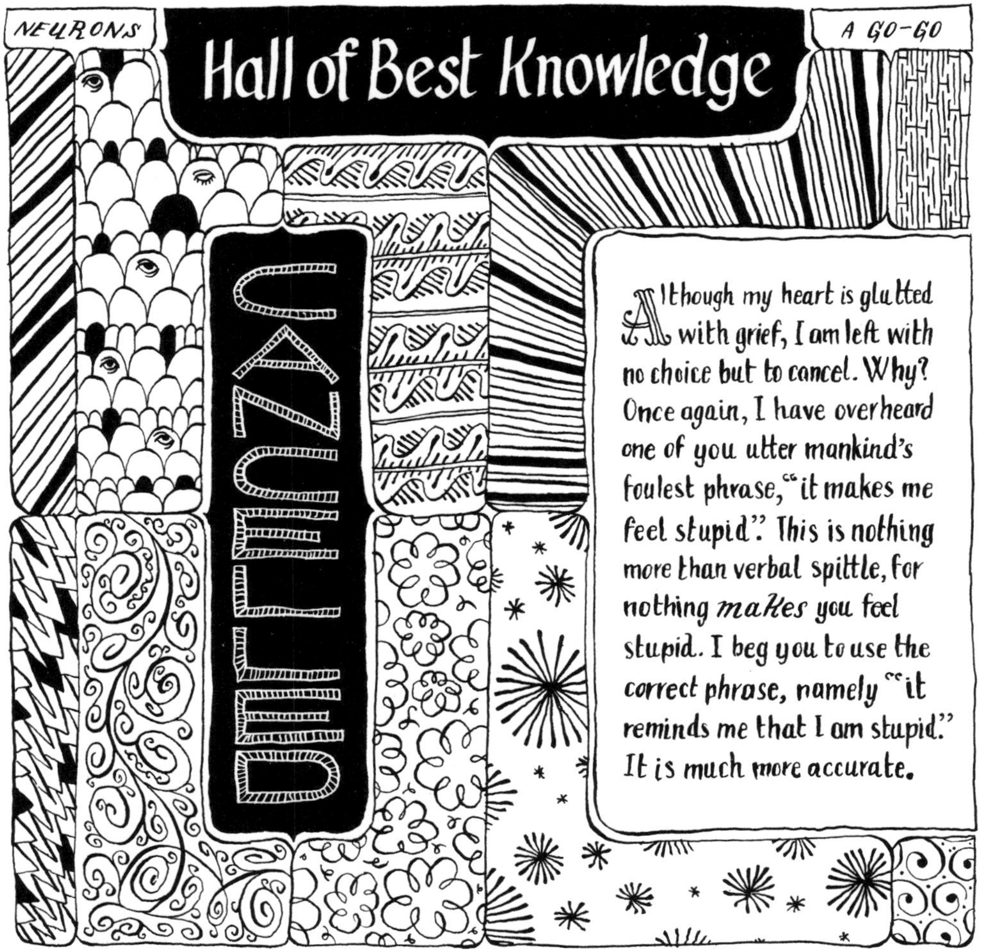
NEURONS
Hall of Best Knowledge
A GO-GO
CANCELLED
Although my heart is glutted with grief, I am left with no choice but to cancel. Why? Once again, I have overheard one of you utter mankind's foulest phrase, "it makes me feel stupid". This is nothing more than verbal spittle, for nothing *makes* you feel stupid. I beg you to use the correct phrase, namely "it reminds me that I am stupid." It is much more accurate.

HALL OF BEST KNOWLEDGE

SEE BELOW

How do we become who we are? Do we carefully and consciously choose our "Self," or are we but balls of tape tumbling down a filthy hallway, picking up HAIR, DUST, FINGERNAILS, EYELASHES, BUG CARCASSES, CRUMBS and other dross? Are we

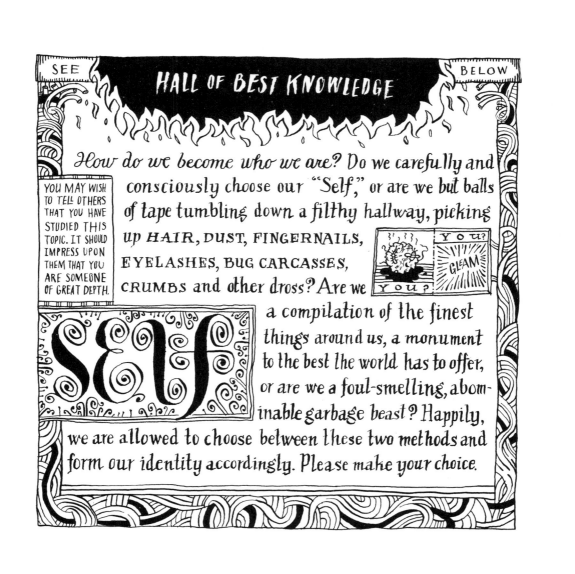

YOU MAY WISH TO TELL OTHERS THAT YOU HAVE STUDIED THIS TOPIC. IT SHOULD IMPRESS UPON THEM THAT YOU ARE SOMEONE OF GREAT DEPTH.

a compilation of the finest things around us, a monument to the best the world has to offer, or are we a foul-smelling, abominable garbage beast? Happily, we are allowed to choose between these two methods and form our identity accordingly. Please make your choice.

LIKE A
Hall of Best Knowledge
PRISM!
It hardly needs mentioning that riding a pony is no intellectual triumph, but just look at the little scene that forms when my broth... when SOMEONE trots but a few steps! Judging by the moon-eyed gaggle of giggling girls, one would think that the person astride the beast had made a clever point or disproved some long-held theory — both of which I have done — when actually they've done nothing more than wobble around atop a miniature horse. I have yet to receive that manner of attention for any of the hard-fought breakthroughs I have made, and I can tell you without hesitation that I do not wish to, not in the least. If the riding of a pony is so fantastic, why have I never read of any reknowned pony-riding genius? It is because such a person does not exist, making it a foolish waste of time unworthy of attention.
PONY
PONY
PONY
PONY
PONY

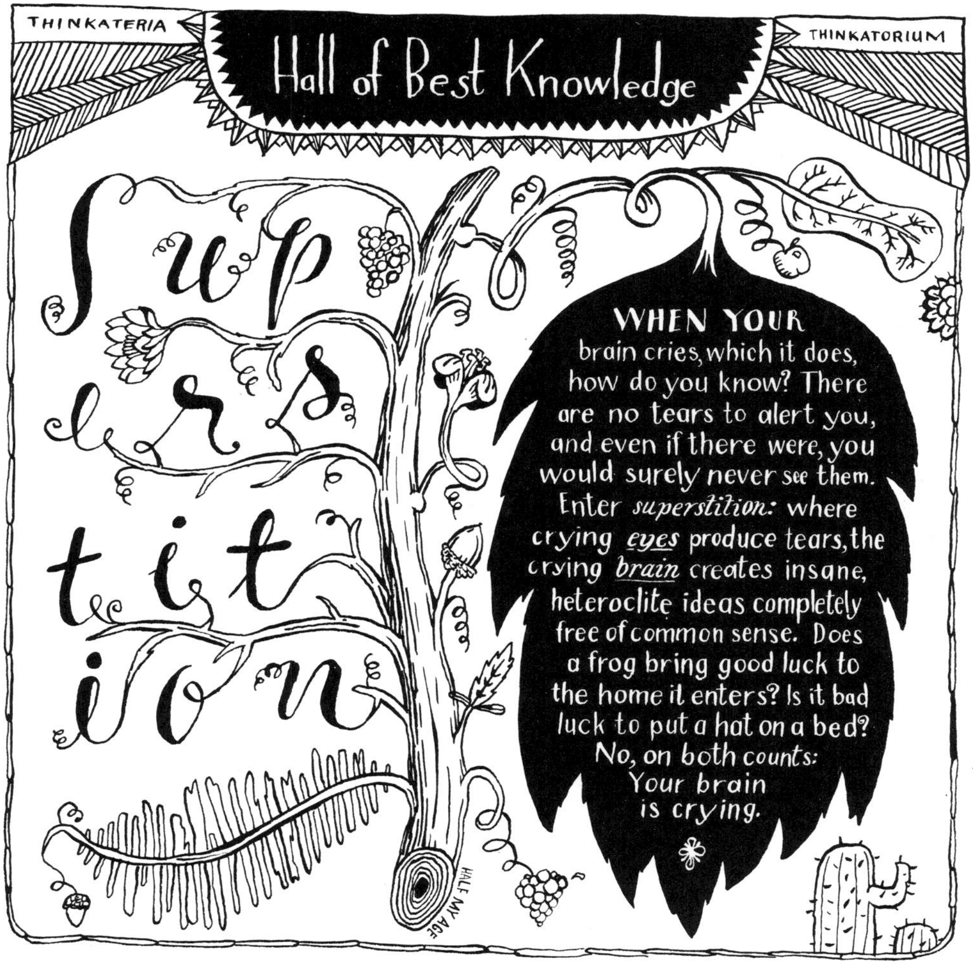
THINKATERIA
Hall of Best Knowledge
THINKATORIUM
Superstition
WHEN YOUR brain cries, which it does, how do you know? There are no tears to alert you, and even if there were, you would surely never see them. Enter *superstition:* where crying eyes produce tears, the crying brain creates insane, heteroclite ideas completely free of common sense. Does a frog bring good luck to the home it enters? Is it bad luck to put a hat on a bed? No, on both counts: Your brain is crying.
HALF MY AGE

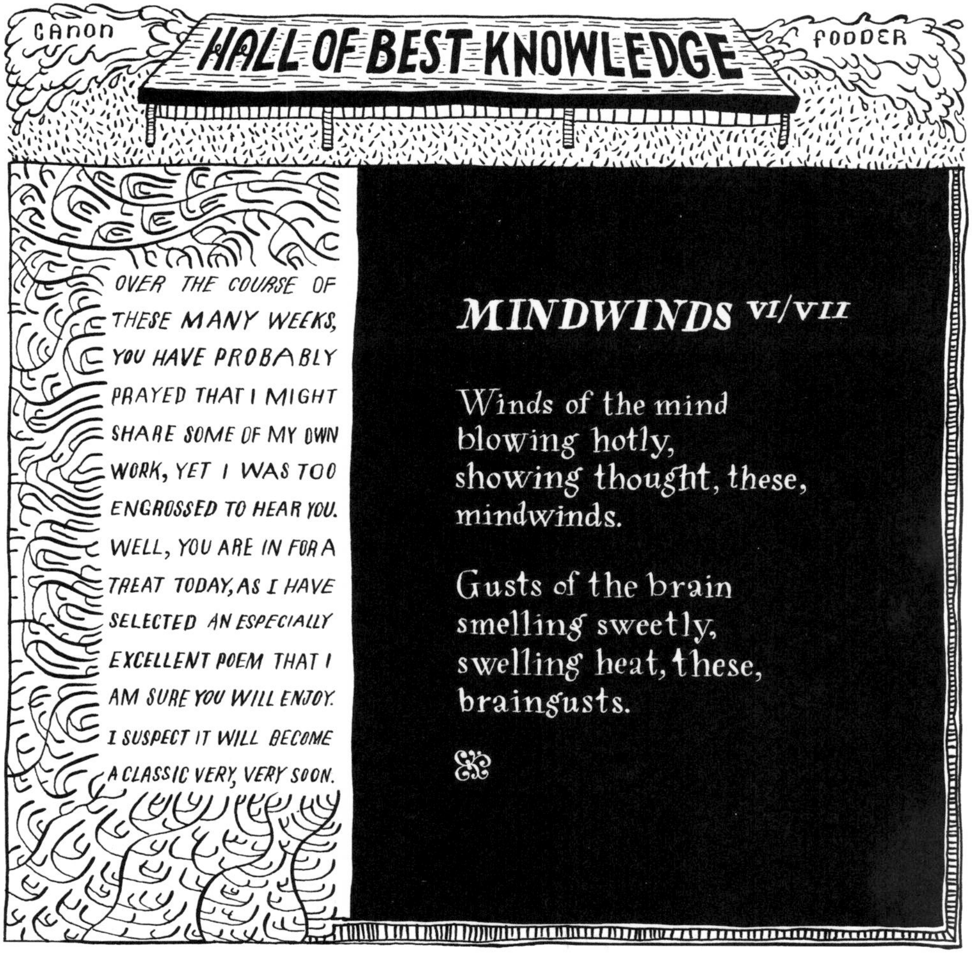

CANON
HALL OF BEST KNOWLEDGE
FODDER
OVER THE COURSE OF THESE MANY WEEKS, YOU HAVE PROBABLY PRAYED THAT I MIGHT SHARE SOME OF MY OWN WORK, YET I WAS TOO ENGROSSED TO HEAR YOU. WELL, YOU ARE IN FOR A TREAT TODAY, AS I HAVE SELECTED AN ESPECIALLY EXCELLENT POEM THAT I AM SURE YOU WILL ENJOY. I SUSPECT IT WILL BECOME A CLASSIC VERY, VERY SOON.
MINDWINDS VI/VII
Winds of the mind
blowing hotly,
showing thought, these,
mindwinds.
Gusts of the brain
smelling sweetly,
swelling heat, these,
braingusts.

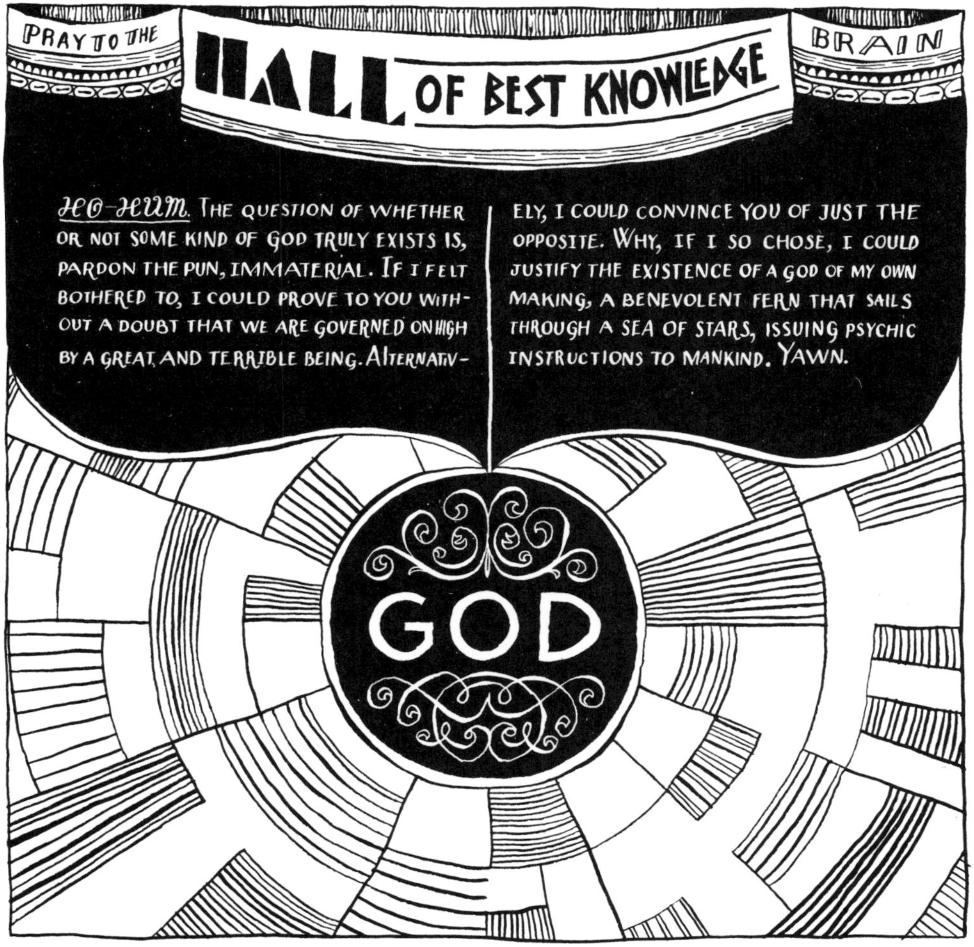
PRAY TO THE
HALL OF BEST KNOWLEDGE
BRAIN
HO-HUM. THE QUESTION OF WHETHER OR NOT SOME KIND OF GOD TRULY EXISTS IS, PARDON THE PUN, IMMATERIAL. IF I FELT BOTHERED TO, I COULD PROVE TO YOU WITHOUT A DOUBT THAT WE ARE GOVERNED ON HIGH BY A GREAT AND TERRIBLE BEING. ALTERNATIVELY, I COULD CONVINCE YOU OF JUST THE OPPOSITE. WHY, IF I SO CHOSE, I COULD JUSTIFY THE EXISTENCE OF A GOD OF MY OWN MAKING, A BENEVOLENT FERN THAT SAILS THROUGH A SEA OF STARS, ISSUING PSYCHIC INSTRUCTIONS TO MANKIND. YAWN.
GOD

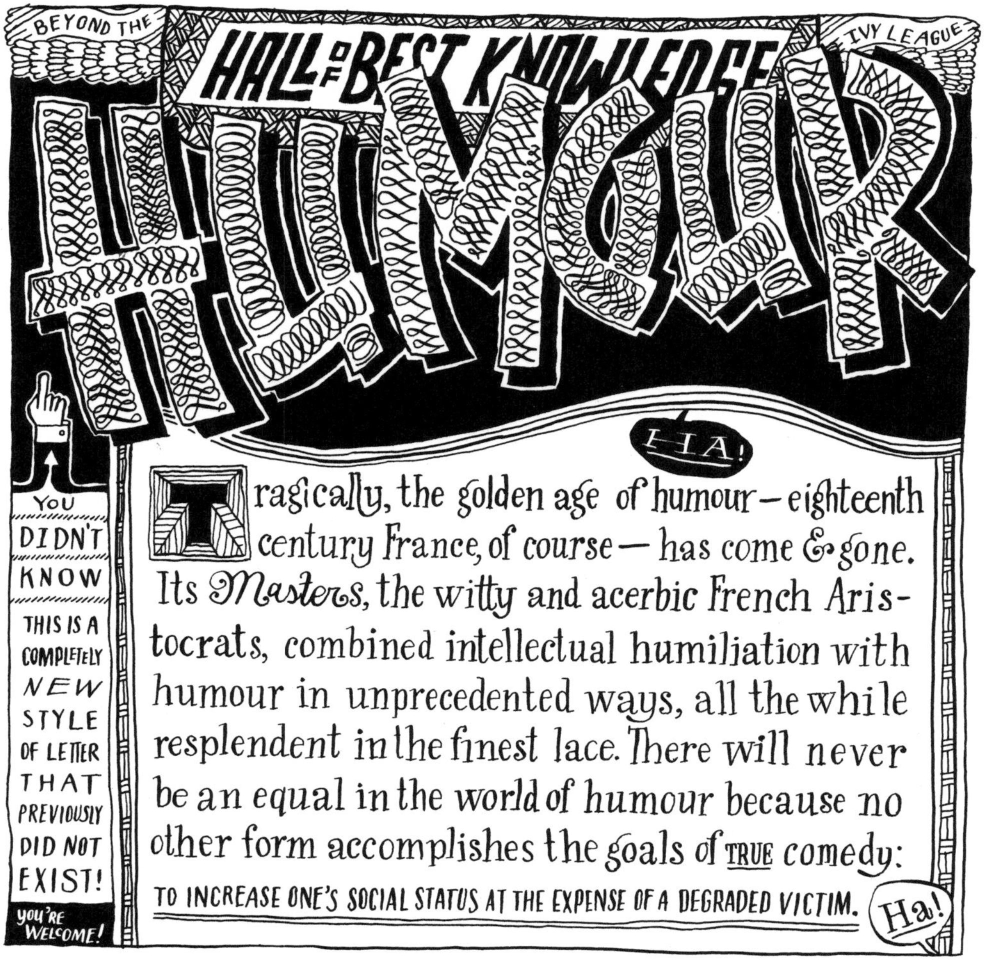
BEYOND THE
IVY LEAGUE
HALL OF BEST KNOWLEDGE
HUMOUR
HA!
Tragically, the golden age of humour — eighteenth century France, of course — has come & gone. Its Masters, the witty and acerbic French Aristocrats, combined intellectual humiliation with humour in unprecedented ways, all the while resplendent in the finest lace. There will never be an equal in the world of humour because no other form accomplishes the goals of TRUE comedy:
TO INCREASE ONE'S SOCIAL STATUS AT THE EXPENSE OF A DEGRADED VICTIM.
Ha!
YOU DIDN'T KNOW
THIS IS A COMPLETELY NEW STYLE OF LETTER THAT PREVIOUSLY DID NOT EXIST!
YOU'RE WELCOME!

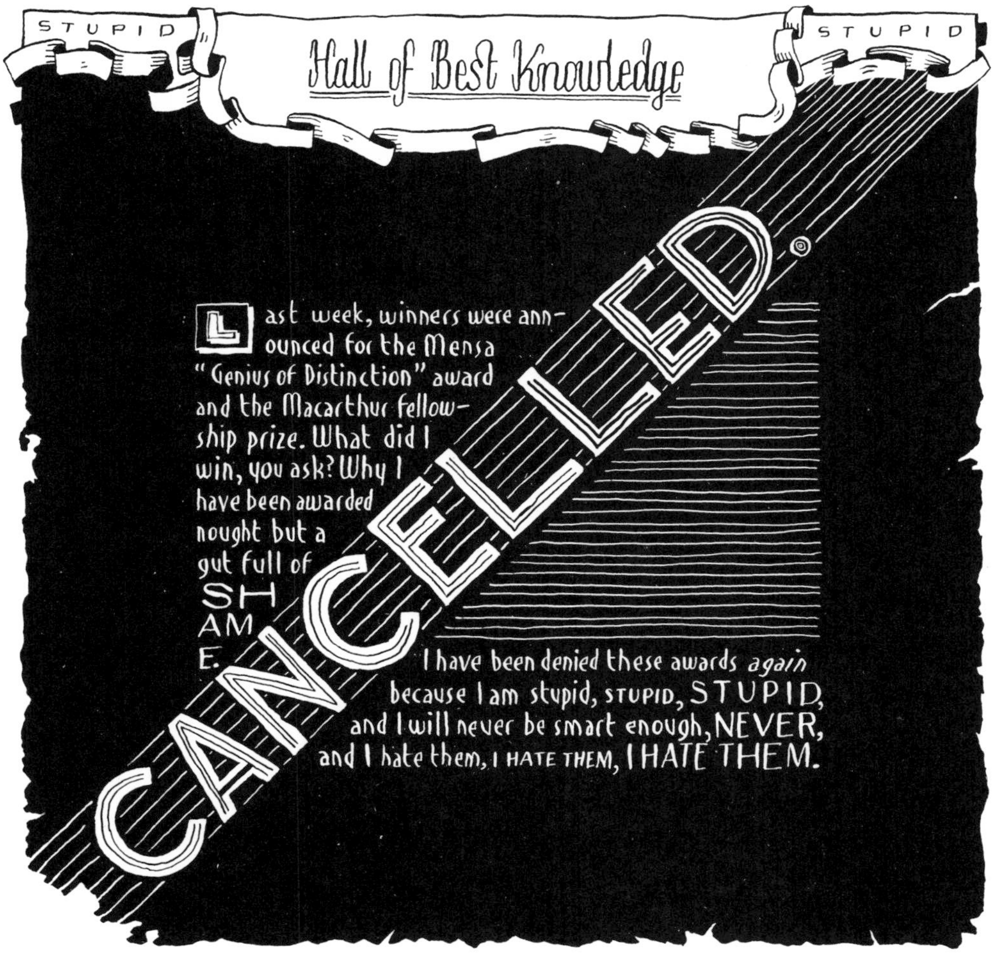
STUPID
Hall of Best Knowledge
STUPID
CANCELLED®
Last week, winners were announced for the Mensa "Genius of Distinction" award and the Macarthur fellowship prize. What did I win, you ask? Why I have been awarded nought but a gut full of SHAME.
I have been denied these awards *again* because I am stupid, STUPID, STUPID, and I will never be smart enough, NEVER, and I hate them, I HATE THEM, I HATE THEM.

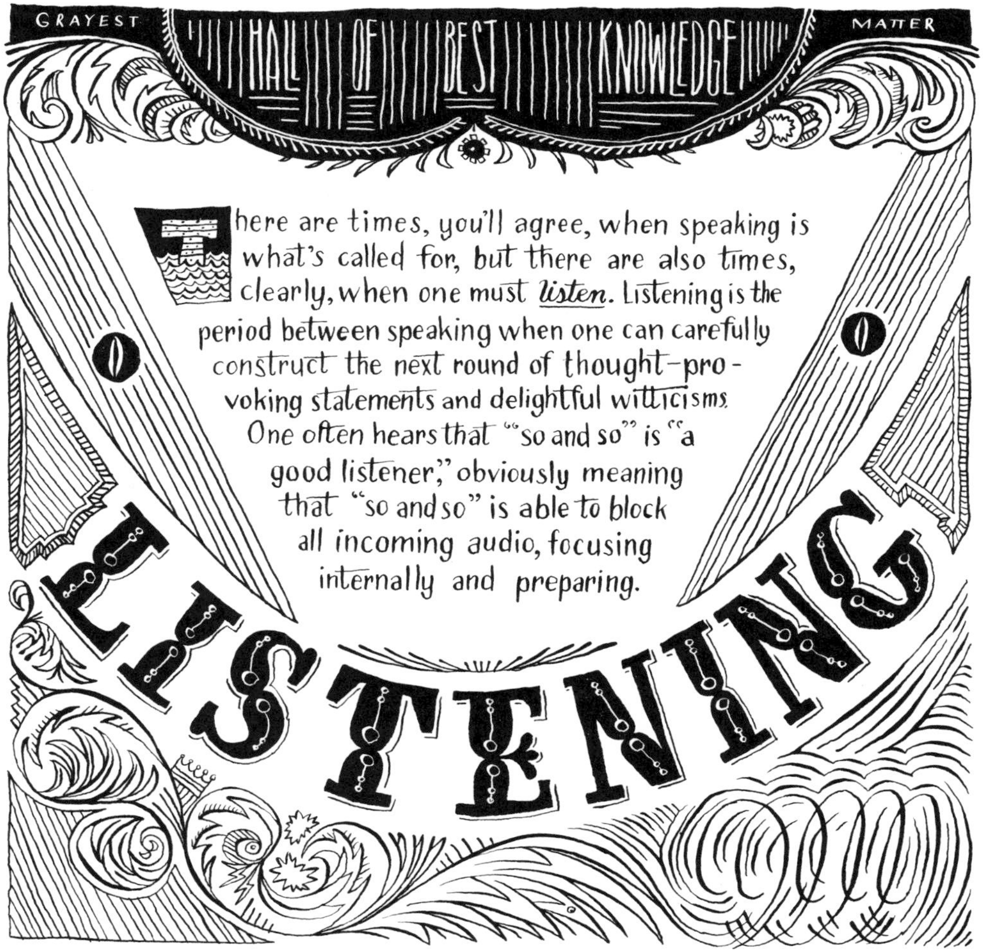
GRAYEST
HALL OF BEST KNOWLEDGE
MATTER
There are times, you'll agree, when speaking is what's called for, but there are also times, clearly, when one must listen. Listening is the period between speaking when one can carefully construct the next round of thought-provoking statements and delightful witticisms. One often hears that "so and so" is "a good listener," obviously meaning that "so and so" is able to block all incoming audio, focusing internally and preparing.
LISTENING

HALL OF BEST KNOWLEDGE

ORIGINALITY

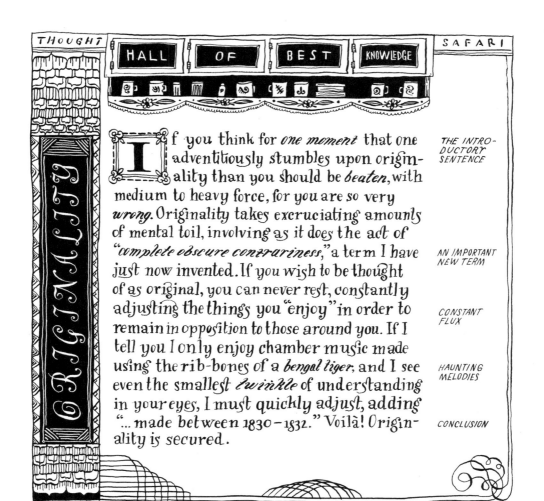

If you think for *one moment* that one adventitiously stumbles upon originality than you should be *beaten*, with medium to heavy force, for you are so very *wrong*. Originality takes excruciating amounts of mental toil, involving as it does the act of *"complete obscure contrariness,"* a term I have just now invented. If you wish to be thought of as original, you can never rest, constantly adjusting the things you "enjoy" in order to remain in opposition to those around you. If I tell you I only enjoy chamber music made using the rib-bones of a *bengal tiger*, and I see even the smallest *twinkle* of understanding in your eyes, I must quickly adjust, adding "...made between 1830–1832." Voilà! Originality is secured.

THE INTRODUCTORY SENTENCE

AN IMPORTANT NEW TERM

CONSTANT FLUX

HAUNTING MELODIES

CONCLUSION

Ha Haaa

Ahh-haha

Hall of Best Knowledge

EPISTEMOLOGY

100 AROUND THE POLE | 50 TOUCHING THE POLE | 20 OTHER | EXCELLENT THROW

Do you _REALLY_ not know what this is? Hahahaha hahaha, ohhhhhhhhhhahahaHAHA, oh hohooooaaaaAHHAHAHAHAA ha, ha, oh, my _my_. AHEM. I'm so very sorry, it's just that I, I, ha, hahaa aaaha HAHA—HAHA—haha ahhaha... I had thought _everyone_ knew this concept, but, but, ha, ha, HA, HAA HAHAHAHA—EEEEEE HEEEE—OHHHHHHHH... Ok. Okay. OKAY. Now, I had thought this was commonly known... but HAHAAAHAHaaaahaha

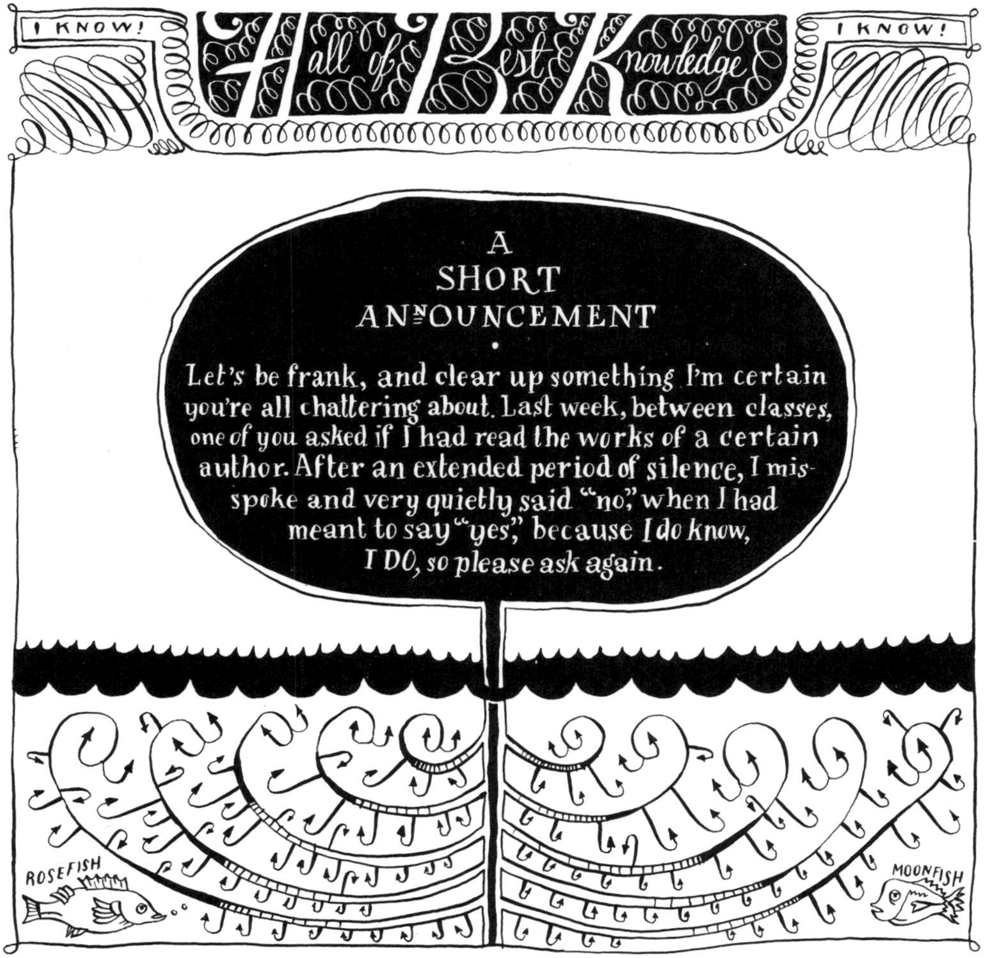
I KNOW!
Hall of Best Knowledge
I KNOW!
A SHORT ANNOUNCEMENT
Let's be frank, and clear up something I'm certain you're all chattering about. Last week, between classes, one of you asked if I had read the works of a certain author. After an extended period of silence, I mis-spoke and very quietly said "no," when I had meant to say "yes," because I do know, I DO, so please ask again.
ROSEFISH
MOONFISH

Hall of Best Knowledge

POOR

INSTINCTS

Each year, as Spring pries open winter's talons, something magical takes place. Spring is the intellectual's season: the landscape bursts with vibrant metaphor and fragrant literary themes, an ideal context for discussion, conversation and poetry. Why, it was Spring that stimulated KEATS, BALZAC & OWEN to create some of our most cherished literary treasures! But what do most of you do? You kneel down in the dirt like an animal and you *sniff the flowers*. No discussion, no poetry, just *sniffing*. Sigh.

SPRING

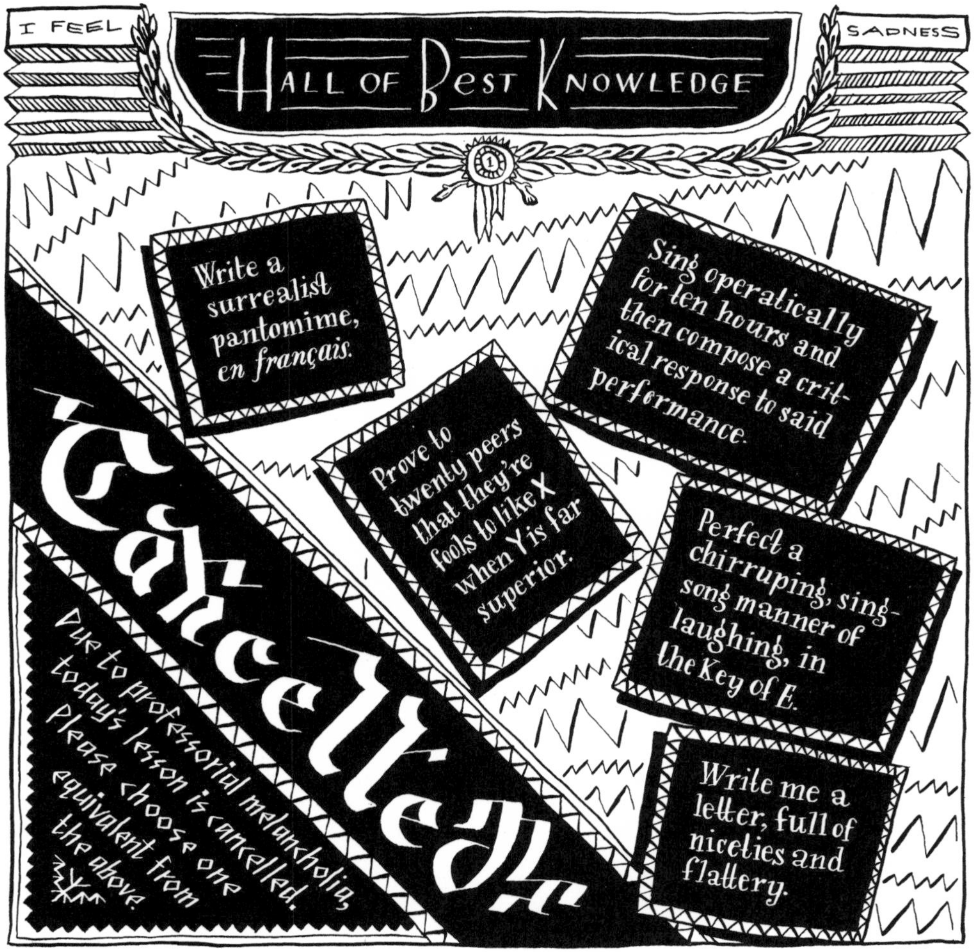
I FEEL
HALL OF BEST KNOWLEDGE
SADNESS
Write a surrealist pantomime, en français.
Sing operatically for ten hours and then compose a critical response to said performance.
Prove to twenty peers that they're fools to like X when Y is far superior.
Perfect a chirruping, sing-song manner of laughing, in the Key of E.
Write me a letter, full of niceties and flattery.
Cancelled.
Due to professorial melancholia, today's lesson is cancelled. Please choose one equivalent from the above.

HALL OF BEST KNOWLEDGE

SOLITUDE

The act of sequestering oneself, it may surprise you, is thought of by many as an airless cavern whose wetted walls crawl with foul blooms of loneliness. Quite the opposite. In actuality, solitude is a hot sugared spring, bursting forth from fertile, rose-adorned soil upon which the sweetest of berries grow.

SEE CHART AT RIGHT.

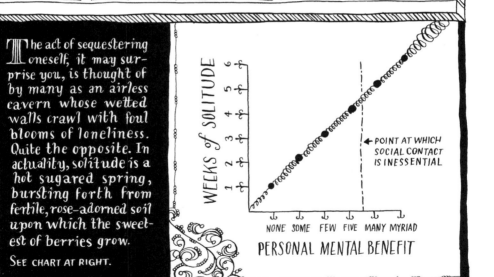

WEEKS OF SOLITUDE

← POINT AT WHICH SOCIAL CONTACT IS INESSENTIAL

NONE SOME FEW FIVE MANY MYRIAD

PERSONAL MENTAL BENEFIT

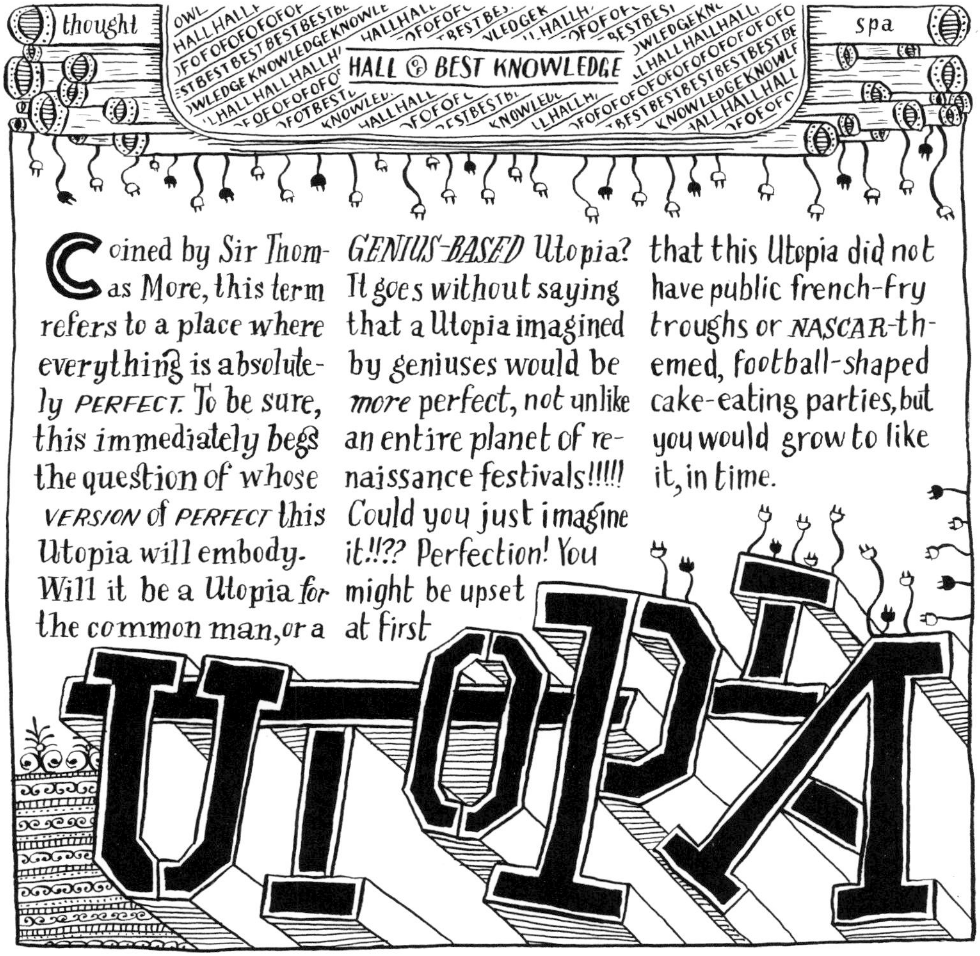
thought
HALL OF BEST KNOWLEDGE
spa
Coined by Sir Thomas More, this term refers to a place where everything is absolutely PERFECT. To be sure, this immediately begs the question of whose VERSION OF PERFECT this Utopia will embody. Will it be a Utopia for the common man, or a GENIUS-BASED Utopia? It goes without saying that a Utopia imagined by geniuses would be more perfect, not unlike an entire planet of renaissance festivals!!!!! Could you just imagine it!!?? Perfection! You might be upset at first that this Utopia did not have public french-fry troughs or NASCAR-themed, football-shaped cake-eating parties, but you would grow to like it, in time.
UTOPIA

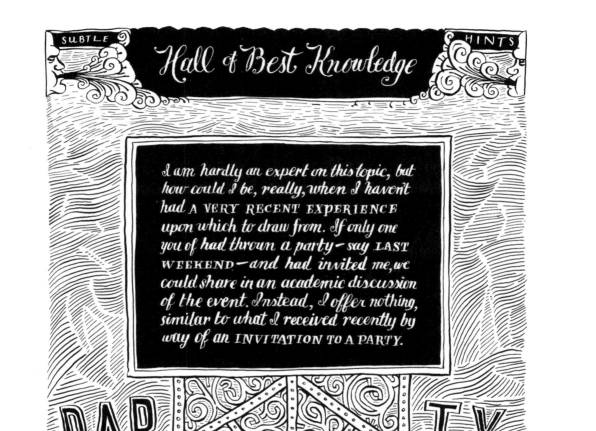

Hall of Best Knowledge

I am hardly an expert on this topic, but how could I be, really, when I haven't had A VERY RECENT EXPERIENCE upon which to draw from. If only one you of had thrown a party — say LAST WEEKEND — and had invited me, we could share in an academic discussion of the event. Instead, I offer nothing, similar to what I received recently by way of an INVITATION TO A PARTY.

PAR TY

RUBY   ENCRUSTED

HALL OF
BEST KNOWLEDGE

WEALTH

It hardly bears mentioning that wealth, beyond all things, is absolutely convenient. Were it not wealth, I would be presently engaged in all manner of vulgar activities—scrubbing this, cooking that—instead of devoting my time to *you*. Why one would choose not to have wealth, I'm not sure. Sloth and dullness, perhaps.

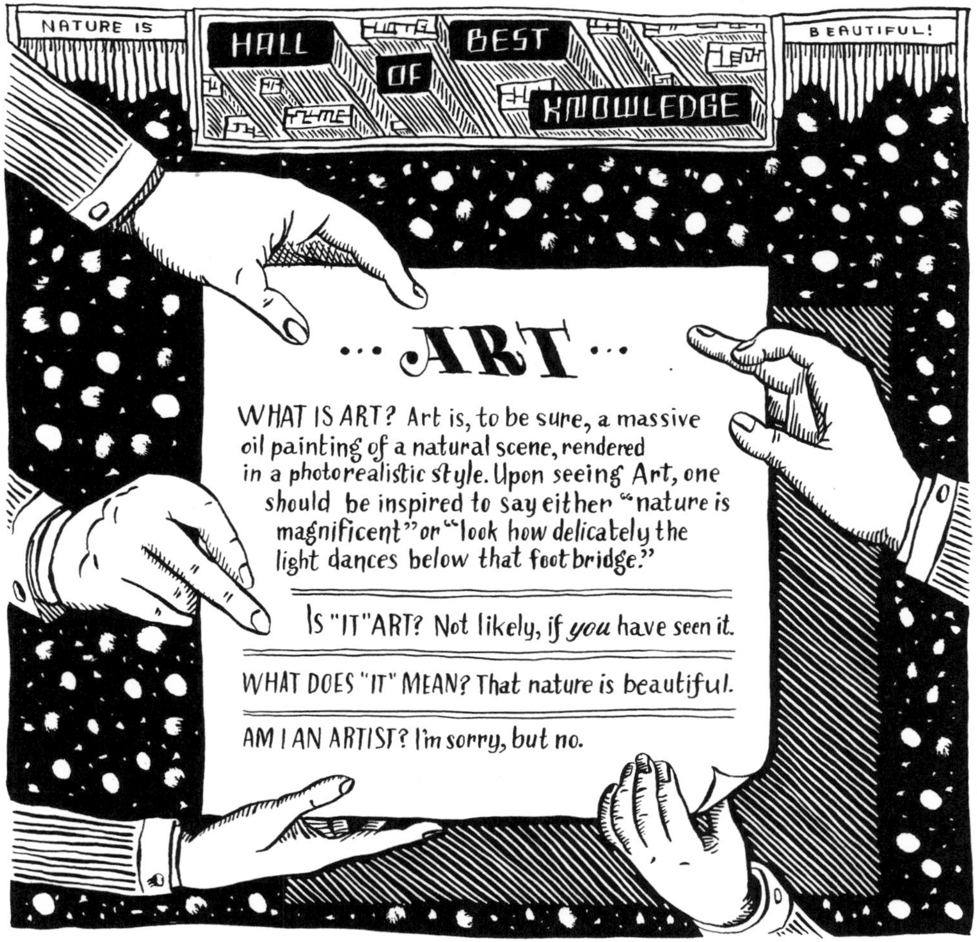
NATURE IS
HALL OF BEST KNOWLEDGE
BEAUTIFUL!
...ART...
WHAT IS ART? Art is, to be sure, a massive oil painting of a natural scene, rendered in a photorealistic style. Upon seeing Art, one should be inspired to say either "nature is magnificent" or "look how delicately the light dances below that foot bridge."
IS "IT" ART? Not likely, if *you* have seen it.
WHAT DOES "IT" MEAN? That nature is beautiful.
AM I AN ARTIST? I'm sorry, but no.

PATENT
Hall of
Best Knowledge
PENDING
LOG AND WEDGE
CLACK VALVE
CROWN WHEEL
CONE PULLEY
CRYOPHORUS
COLLAR
BRUSH WHEEL
HORSES TAIL HAIR
NUT
WEIGHT
PAINTED STUB
DIFFERENTIAL WINDLASS
SPIRAL OF ARCHIMEDES
LATHE CARRIER
TUBULATED RETORT
GOLD HOOK
MAGIC SQUARE
2 7 6
9 5 1
4 3 8
A·RECENT·INVENTION!

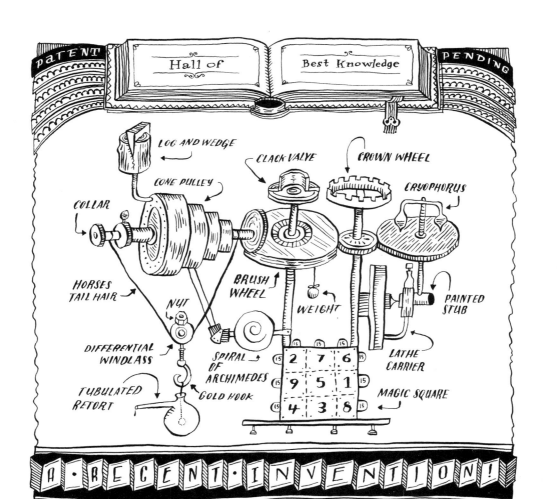

Hall of Best Knowledge

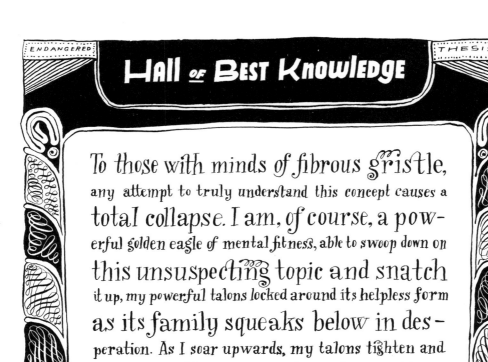

To those with minds of fibrous gristle, any attempt to truly understand this concept causes a total collapse. I am, of course, a powerful golden eagle of mental fitness, able to swoop down on this unsuspecting topic and snatch it up, my powerful talons locked around its helpless form as its family squeaks below in desperation. As I soar upwards, my talons tighten and squeeze the marmot — idea rather — until it gently succumbs. It is then devoured.

ELECTRICITY

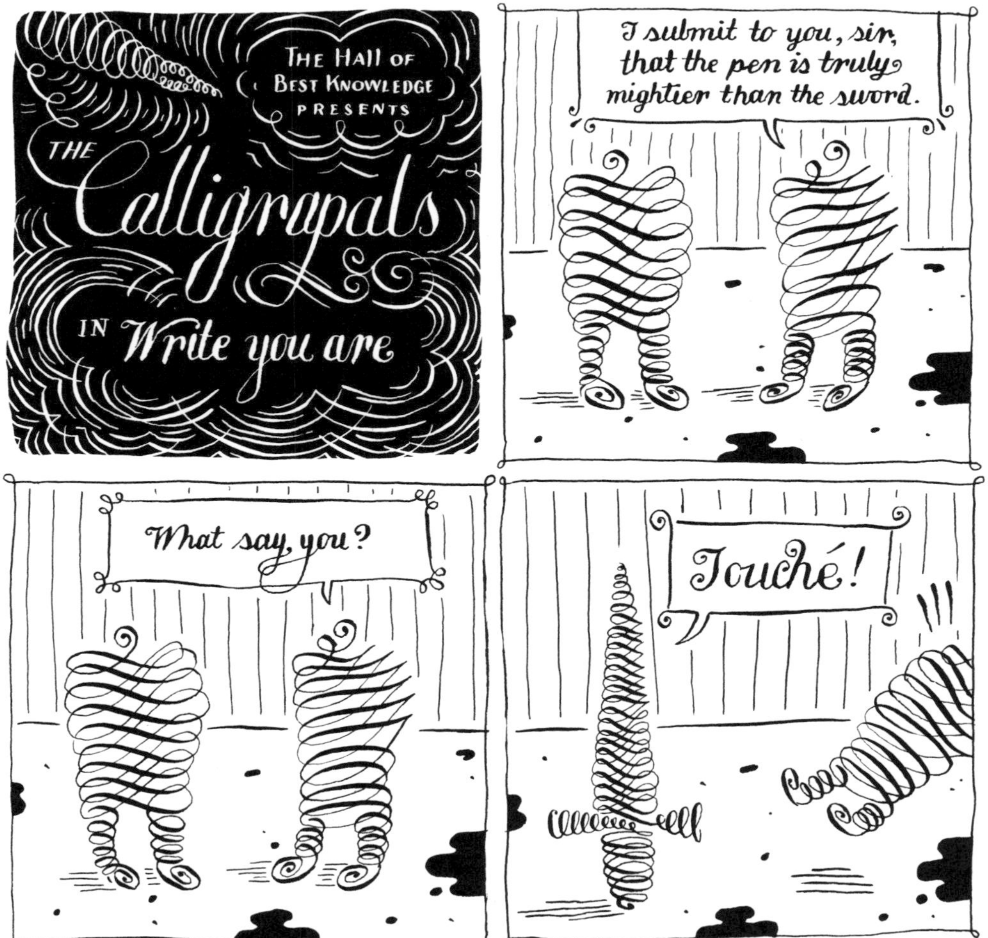
THE HALL OF BEST KNOWLEDGE PRESENTS
THE Callignapals
IN Write you are
I submit to you, sir, that the pen is truly mightier than the sword.
What say, you?
Touché!

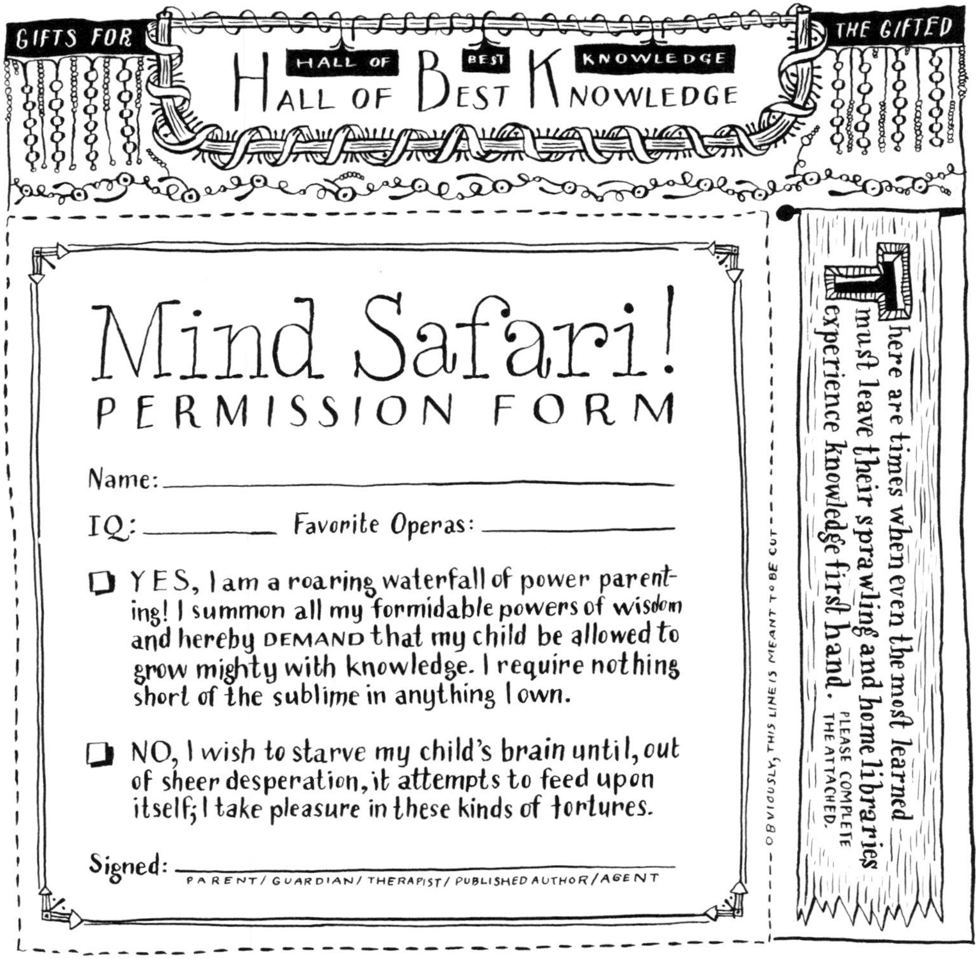
GIFTS FOR
HALL OF BEST KNOWLEDGE
HALL OF BEST KNOWLEDGE
THE GIFTED
Mind Safari!
PERMISSION FORM
Name:
IQ:
Favorite Operas:
YES, I am a roaring waterfall of power parenting! I summon all my formidable powers of wisdom and hereby DEMAND that my child be allowed to grow mighty with knowledge. I require nothing short of the sublime in anything I own.
NO, I wish to starve my child's brain until, out of sheer desperation, it attempts to feed upon itself; I take pleasure in these kinds of tortures.
Signed:
PARENT/GUARDIAN/THERAPIST/PUBLISHED AUTHOR/AGENT
OBVIOUSLY, THIS LINE IS MEANT TO BE CUT
There are times when even the most learned must leave their sprawling and home libraries experience knowledge first hand.
PLEASE COMPLETE THE ATTACHED.

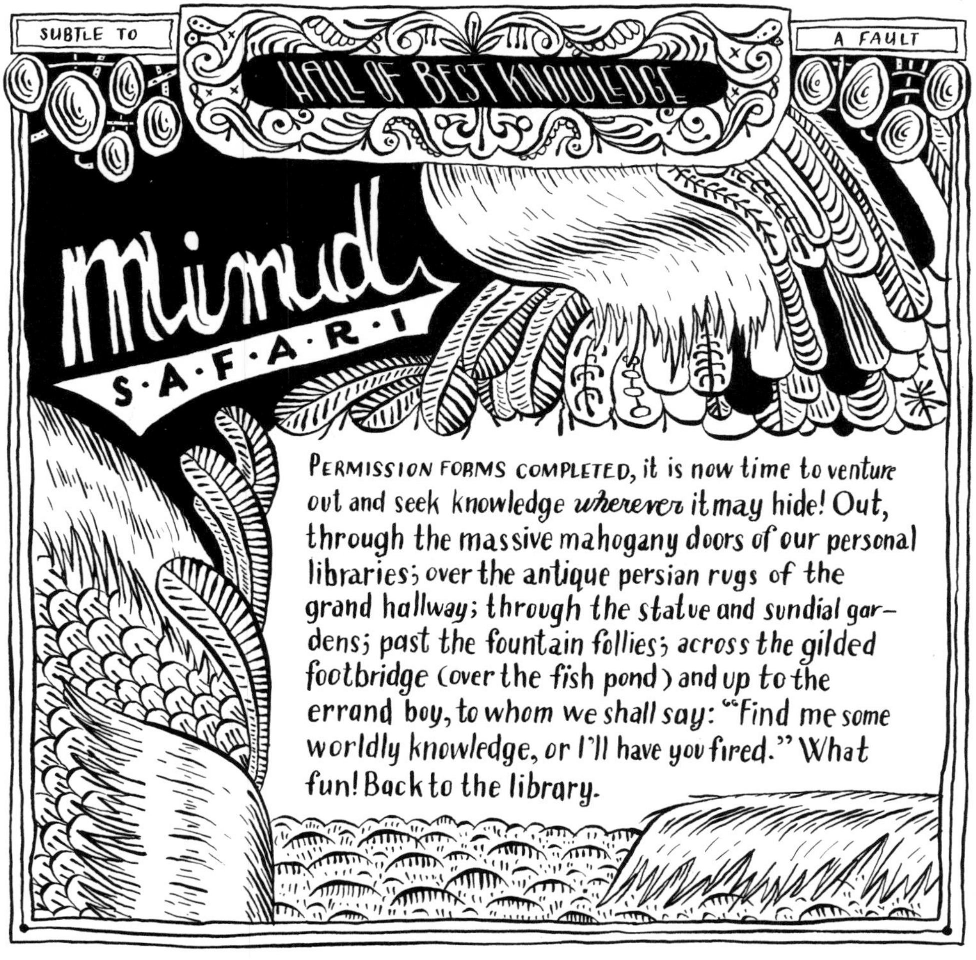
SUBTLE TO
HALL OF BEST KNOWLEDGE
A FAULT
mind
S·A·F·A·R·I
PERMISSION FORMS COMPLETED, it is now time to venture out and seek knowledge wherever it may hide! Out, through the massive mahogany doors of our personal libraries; over the antique persian rugs of the grand hallway; through the statue and sundial gardens; past the fountain follies; across the gilded footbridge (over the fish pond) and up to the errand boy, to whom we shall say: "Find me some worldly knowledge, or I'll have you fired." What fun! Back to the library.

Hall OF Best KNOWLEDGE

ONE YEAR =   3,000,000 IDEAS

BIRTH

What a coincidence, to be sure! Here I am, about to redefine your understanding of yet another complicated topic when it occurs to me that today is MY birthday! Imagine, a lesson on birthdays and my *actual* birthday – on the same day! What are the chances? Having studied entire libraries dedicated to such mathematical probabilities, I can assure you that the chances are LOW. This experience is truly something special, like the combination of an eclipse *and* a meteor shower. To wit, we should discuss this at the party you've surely planned for me.

DAY

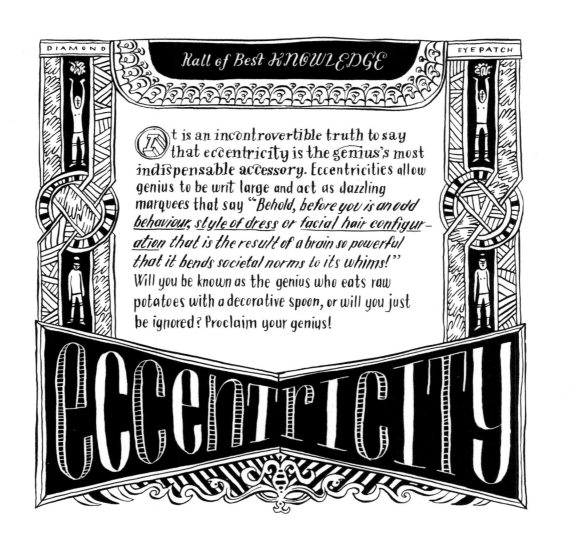

DIAMOND

EYE PATCH

It is an incontrovertible truth to say that eccentricity is the genius's most indispensable accessory. Eccentricities allow genius to be writ large and act as dazzling marquees that say "Behold, before you is an odd _behaviour, style of dress or facial hair configuration_ that is the result of a brain so powerful that it bends societal norms to its whims!" Will you be known as the genius who eats raw potatoes with a decorative spoon, or will you just be ignored? Proclaim your genius!

eccentricity

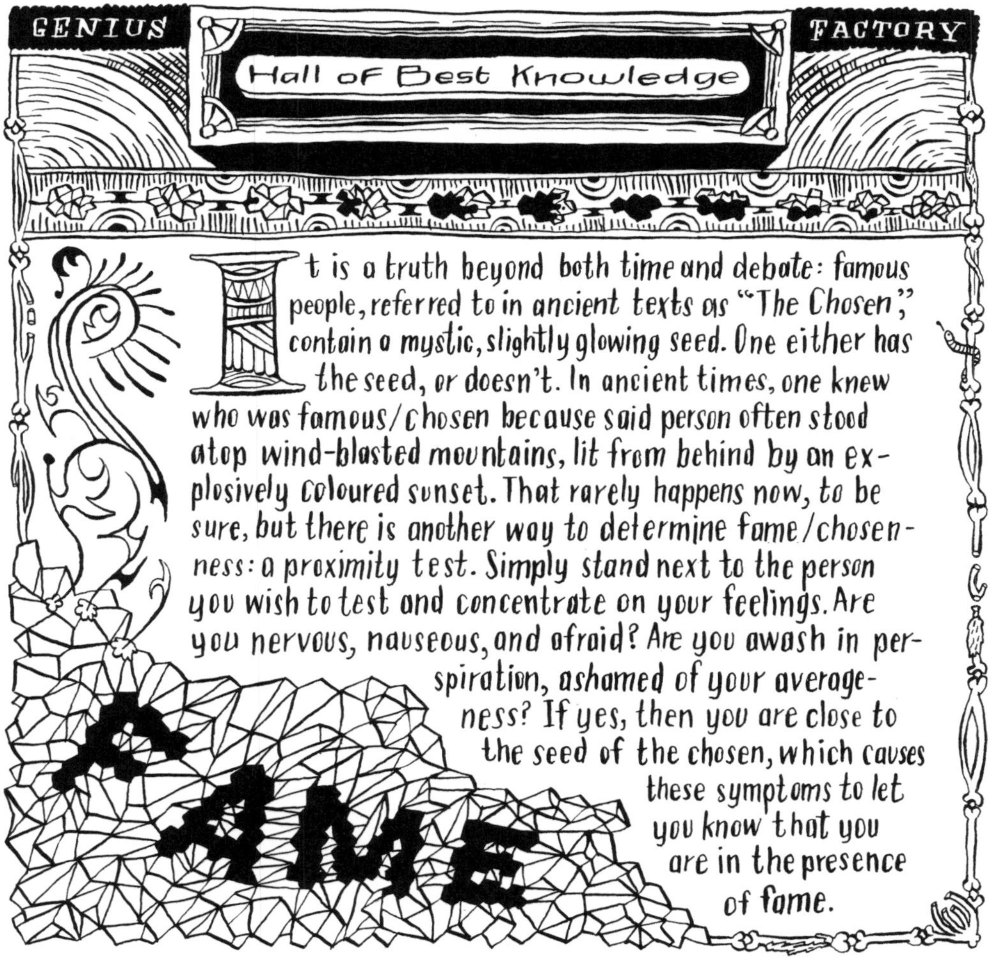
GENIUS
FACTORY
Hall of Best Knowledge
It is a truth beyond both time and debate: famous people, referred to in ancient texts as "The Chosen," contain a mystic, slightly glowing seed. One either has the seed, or doesn't. In ancient times, one knew who was famous/chosen because said person often stood atop wind-blasted mountains, lit from behind by an explosively coloured sunset. That rarely happens now, to be sure, but there is another way to determine fame/chosenness: a proximity test. Simply stand next to the person you wish to test and concentrate on your feelings. Are you nervous, nauseous, and afraid? Are you awash in perspiration, ashamed of your averageness? If yes, then you are close to the seed of the chosen, which causes these symptoms to let you know that you are in the presence of fame.
FAME

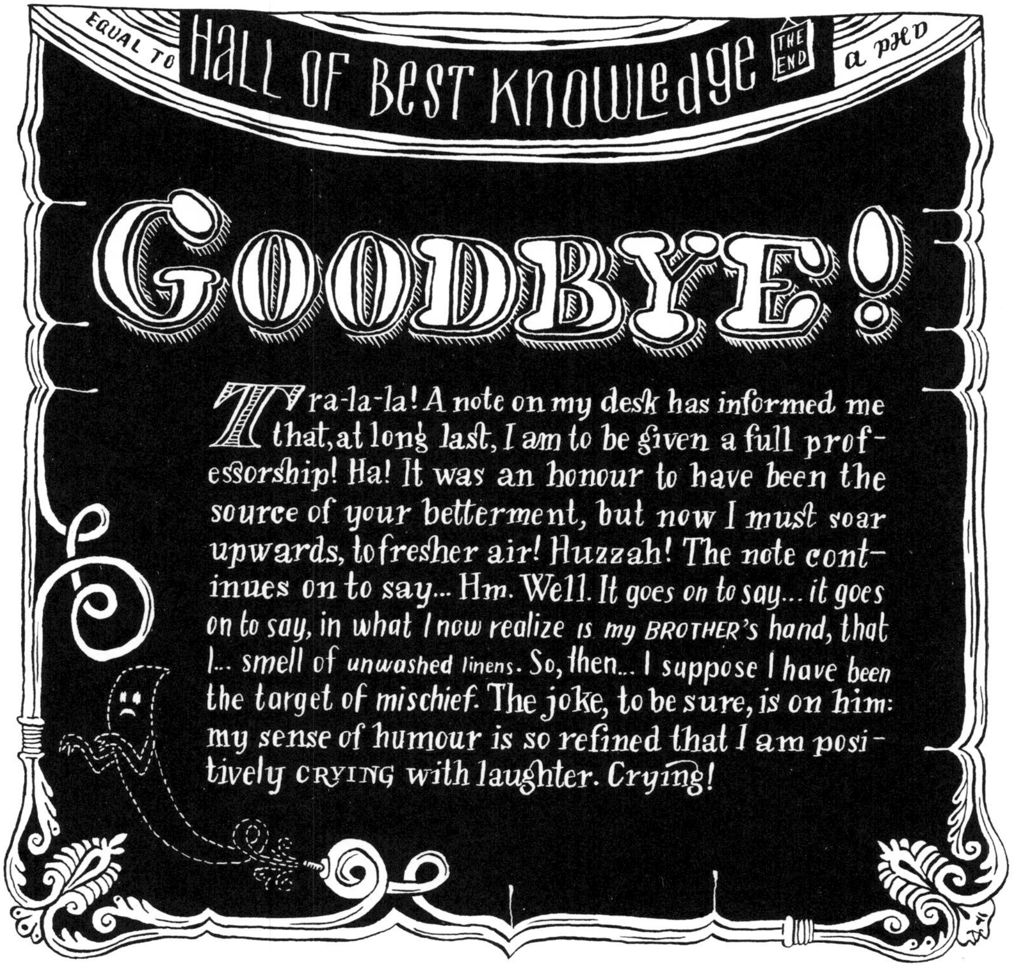

EQUAL TO
HALL OF BEST KNOWLEDGE
THE END
A PHD
GOODBYE!
Tra-la-la! A note on my desk has informed me that, at long last, I am to be given a full professorship! Ha! It was an honour to have been the source of your betterment, but now I must soar upwards, to fresher air! Huzzah! The note continues on to say... Hm. Well. It goes on to say... it goes on to say, in what I now realize is my BROTHER's hand, that I... smell of unwashed linens. So, then... I suppose I have been the target of mischief. The joke, to be sure, is on him: my sense of humour is so refined that I am positively CRYING with laughter. Crying!

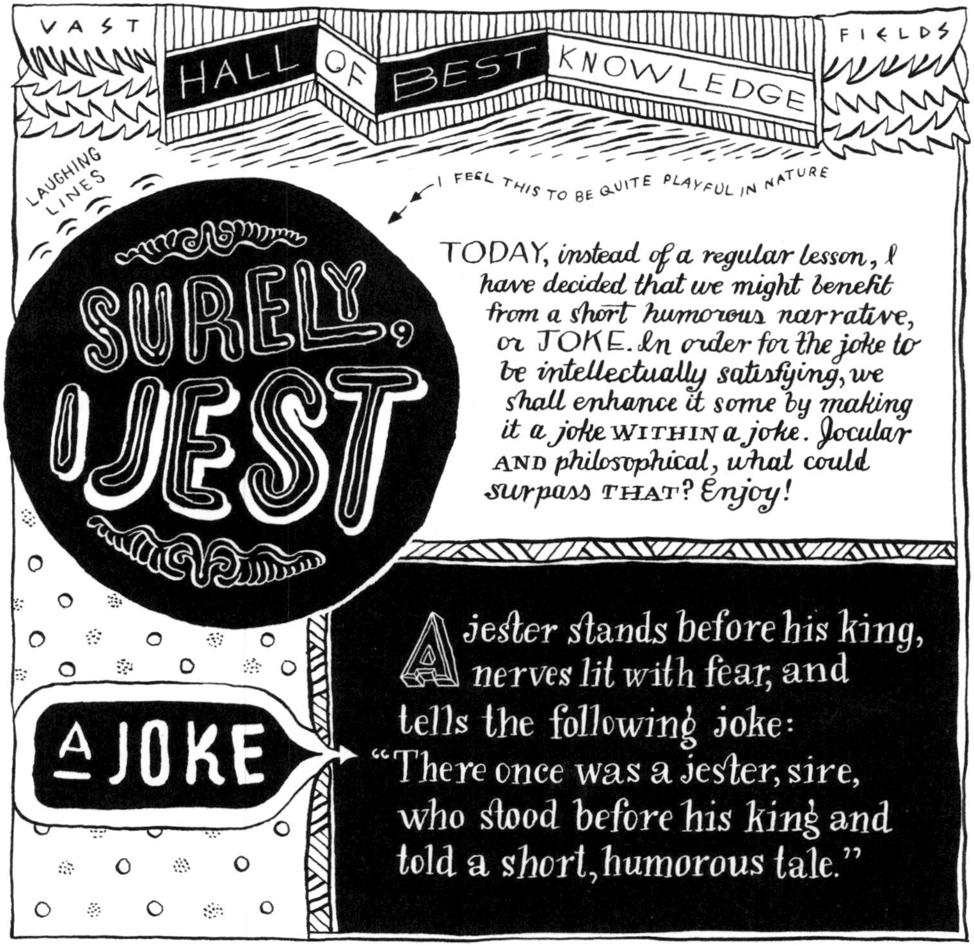
VAST
HALL OF BEST KNOWLEDGE
FIELDS
LAUGHING LINES
I FEEL THIS TO BE QUITE PLAYFUL IN NATURE
SURELY, I JEST
TODAY, instead of a regular lesson, I have decided that we might benefit from a short humorous narrative, or JOKE. In order for the joke to be intellectually satisfying, we shall enhance it some by making it a joke WITHIN a joke. Jocular AND philosophical, what could surpass THAT? Enjoy!
A JOKE
A jester stands before his king, nerves lit with fear, and tells the following joke:
"There once was a jester, sire, who stood before his king and told a short, humorous tale."

FALLOW
FIELDS
Hall of Best Knowledge
CANCELLED
Quite frankly, I haven't the time. My apologies.

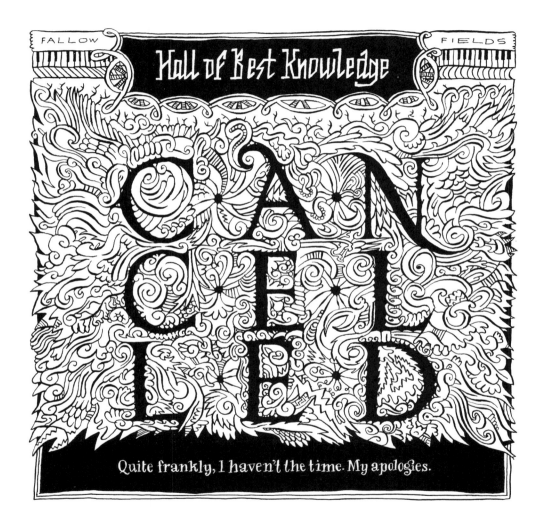

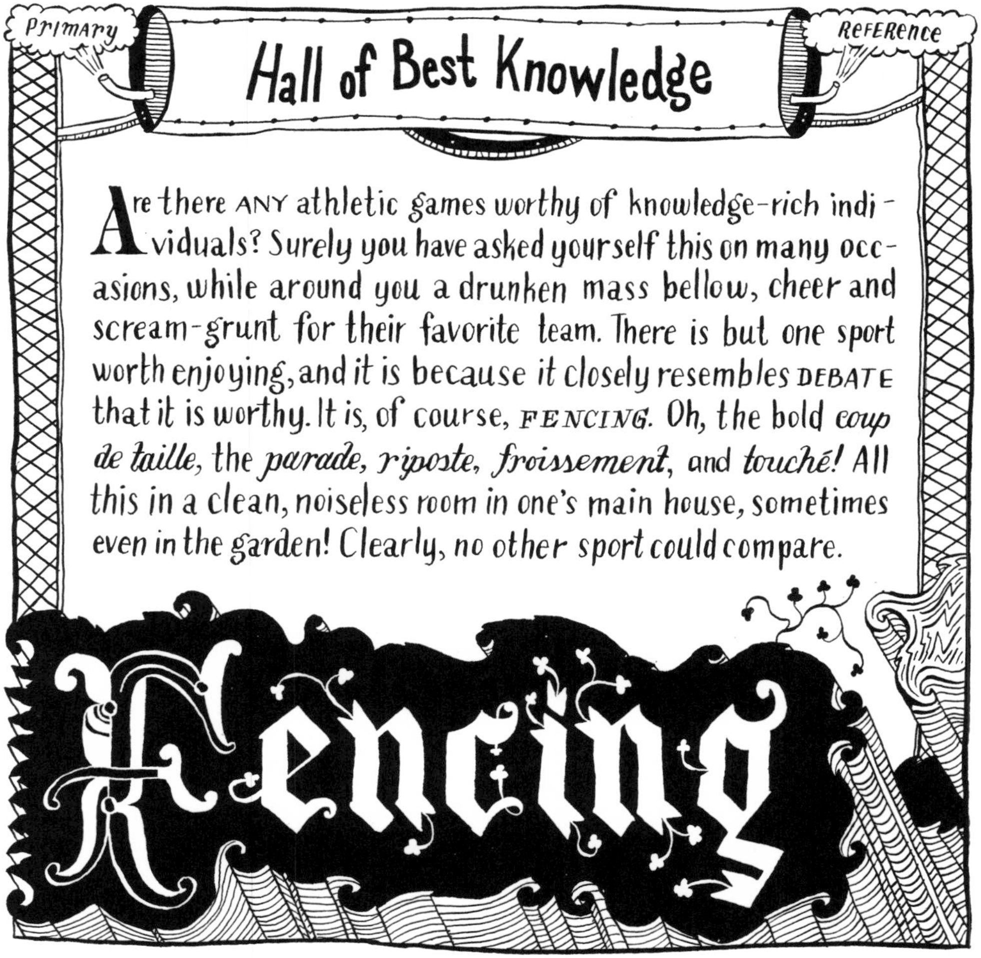
Primary
Reference
Hall of Best Knowledge
Are there ANY athletic games worthy of knowledge-rich individuals? Surely you have asked yourself this on many occasions, while around you a drunken mass bellow, cheer and scream-grunt for their favorite team. There is but one sport worth enjoying, and it is because it closely resembles DEBATE that it is worthy. It is, of course, FENCING. Oh, the bold *coup de taille*, the *parade*, *riposte*, *froissement*, and *touché!* All this in a clean, noiseless room in one's main house, sometimes even in the garden! Clearly, no other sport could compare.
Fencing

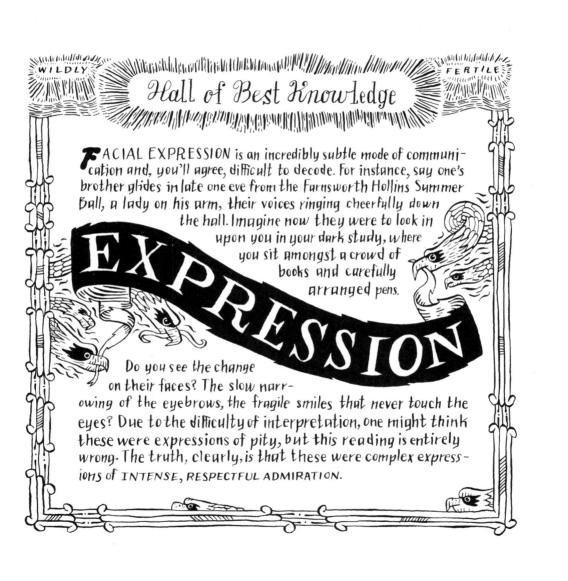

Hall of Best Knowledge

FACIAL EXPRESSION is an incredibly subtle mode of communi-cation and, you'll agree, difficult to decode. For instance, say one's brother glides in late one eve from the Farnsworth Hollins Summer Ball, a lady on his arm, their voices ringing cheerfully down the hall. Imagine now they were to look in upon you in your dark study, where you sit amongst a crowd of books and carefully arranged pens.

EXPRESSION

Do you see the change on their faces? The slow narr-owing of the eyebrows, the fragile smiles that never touch the eyes? Due to the difficulty of interpretation, one might think these were expressions of pity, but this reading is entirely wrong. The truth, clearly, is that these were complex express-ions of INTENSE, RESPECTFUL ADMIRATION.

SPIRIT of EXCELLENCE

HALL OF BEST KNOWLEDGE

entertainment

To be sure, babies <u>need</u> entertainments whilst confined to a crib. They're unable to make their way to a library, not yet capable of even *basic* conversational latin and must find stimulation elsewhere. *They* can be forgiven for being entranced by a colourful mobile or plush miniaturized animal, but what excuse have *you*? You've replaced the aforementioned infantile appurtenances with television and movies, but I'm convinced you would be just as pleased with, say, a gayly-hued scrap of coloured foil. Oh, how it crinkles so delightfully! My, how it dazzles! You could play with it for *hours*, couldn't you? *Yes you could, yes. Yes. Who could? You! You!* You could, because you are like a baby, obviously.

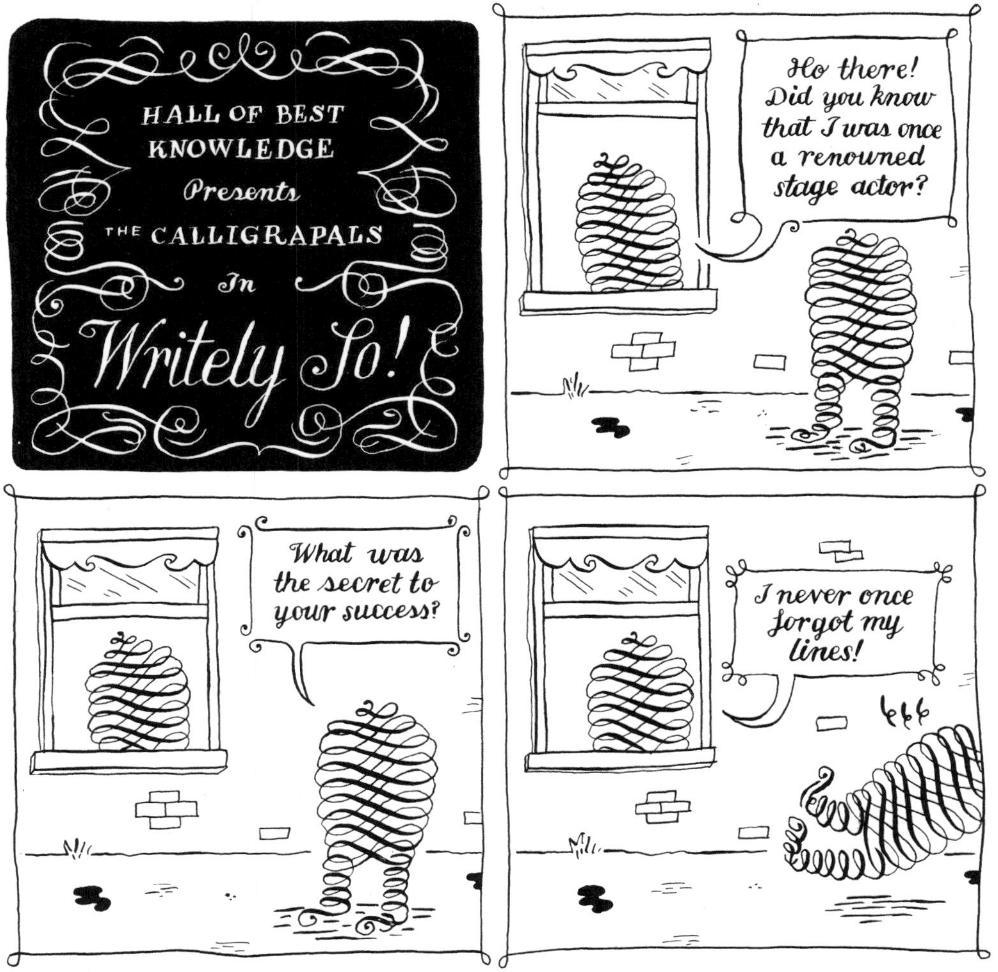
HALL OF BEST KNOWLEDGE
Presents
THE CALLIGRAPALS
In
Writely So!
Ho there! Did you know that I was once a renowned stage actor?
What was the secret to your success?
I never once forgot my lines!

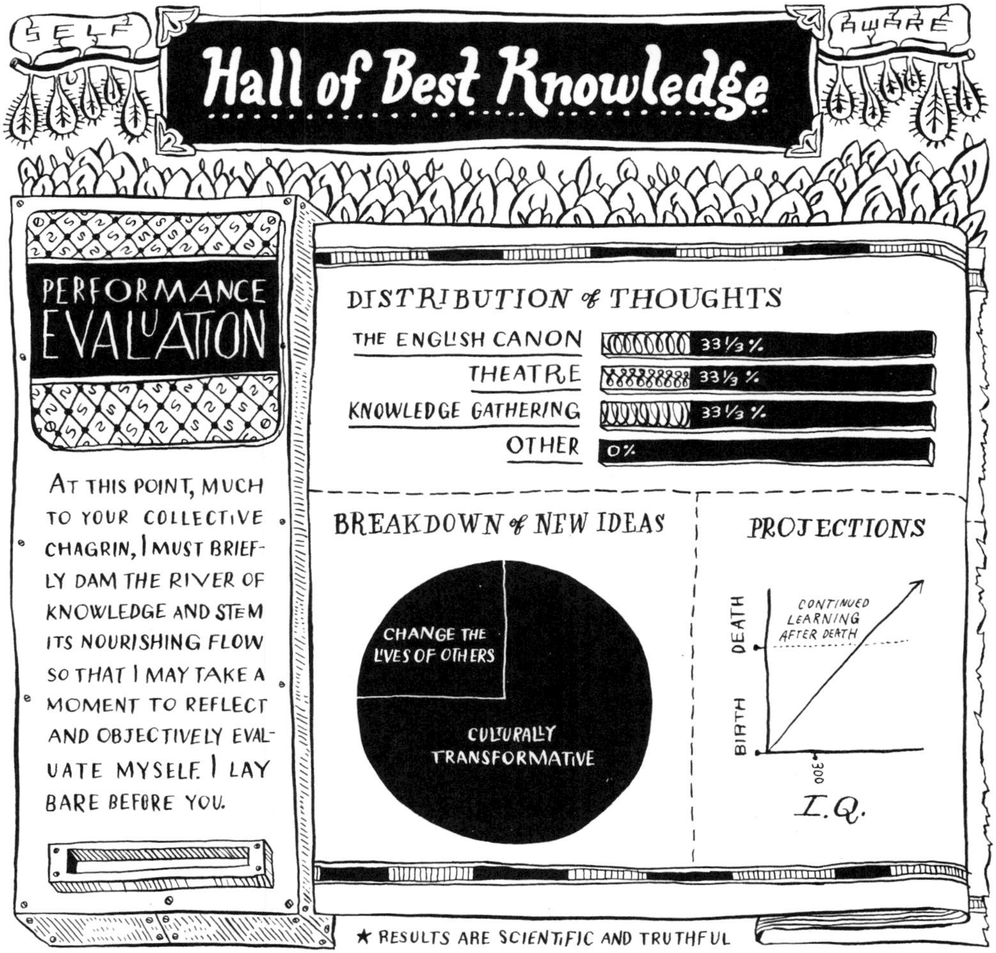
SELF
AWARE
Hall of Best Knowledge
PERFORMANCE EVALUATION
AT THIS POINT, MUCH TO YOUR COLLECTIVE CHAGRIN, I MUST BRIEFLY DAM THE RIVER OF KNOWLEDGE AND STEM ITS NOURISHING FLOW SO THAT I MAY TAKE A MOMENT TO REFLECT AND OBJECTIVELY EVALUATE MYSELF. I LAY BARE BEFORE YOU.
DISTRIBUTION of THOUGHTS
THE ENGLISH CANON
33 1/3 %
THEATRE
33 1/3 %
KNOWLEDGE GATHERING
33 1/3 %
OTHER
0%
BREAKDOWN of NEW IDEAS
CHANGE THE LIVES OF OTHERS
CULTURALLY TRANSFORMATIVE
PROJECTIONS
DEATH
BIRTH
CONTINUED LEARNING AFTER DEATH
300
I.Q.
★ RESULTS ARE SCIENTIFIC AND TRUTHFUL

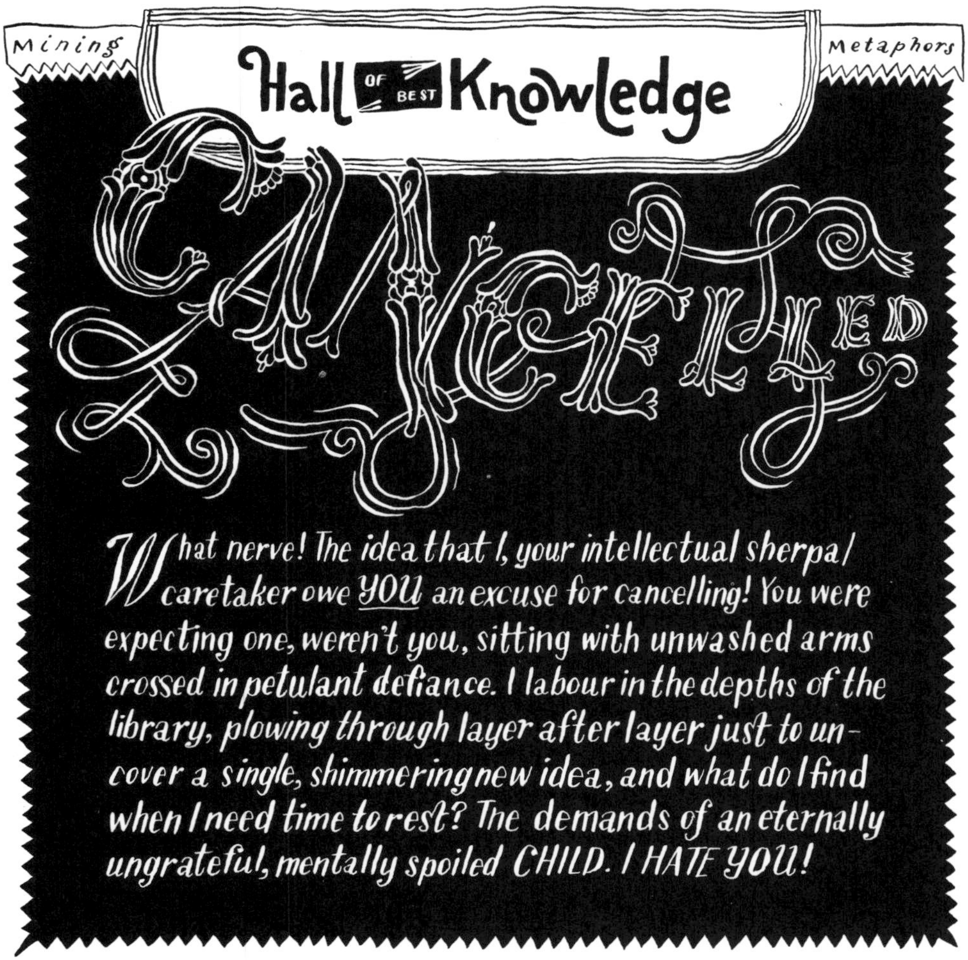
Mining
Hall of Best Knowledge
Metaphors
CANCELLED
What nerve! The idea that I, your intellectual sherpa/caretaker owe YOU an excuse for cancelling! You were expecting one, weren't you, sitting with unwashed arms crossed in petulant defiance. I labour in the depths of the library, plowing through layer after layer just to uncover a single, shimmering new idea, and what do I find when I need time to rest? The demands of an eternally ungrateful, mentally spoiled CHILD. I HATE YOU!

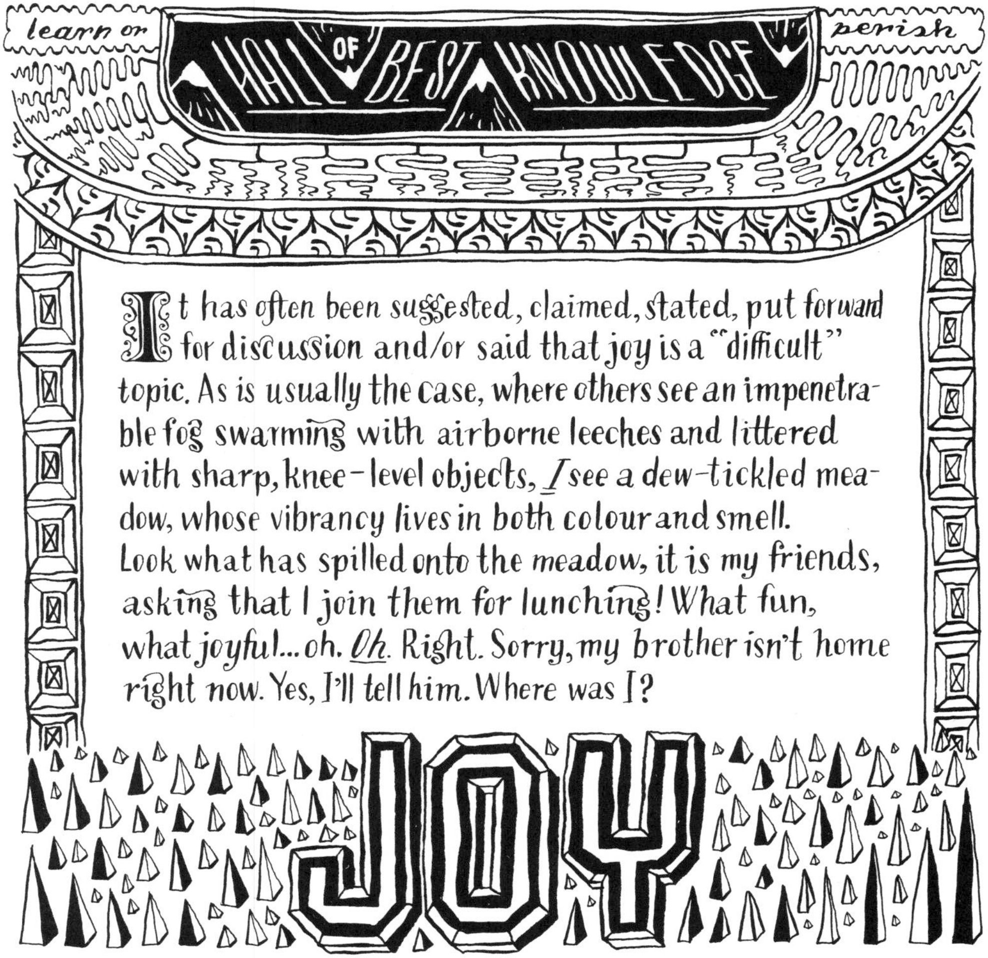
learn or
HALL OF BEST KNOWLEDGE
perish
It has often been suggested, claimed, stated, put forward for discussion and/or said that joy is a "difficult" topic. As is usually the case, where others see an impenetrable fog swarming with airborne leeches and littered with sharp, knee-level objects, I see a dew-tickled meadow, whose vibrancy lives in both colour and smell. Look what has spilled onto the meadow, it is my friends, asking that I join them for lunching! What fun, what joyful... oh. Oh. Right. Sorry, my brother isn't home right now. Yes, I'll tell him. Where was I?
JOY

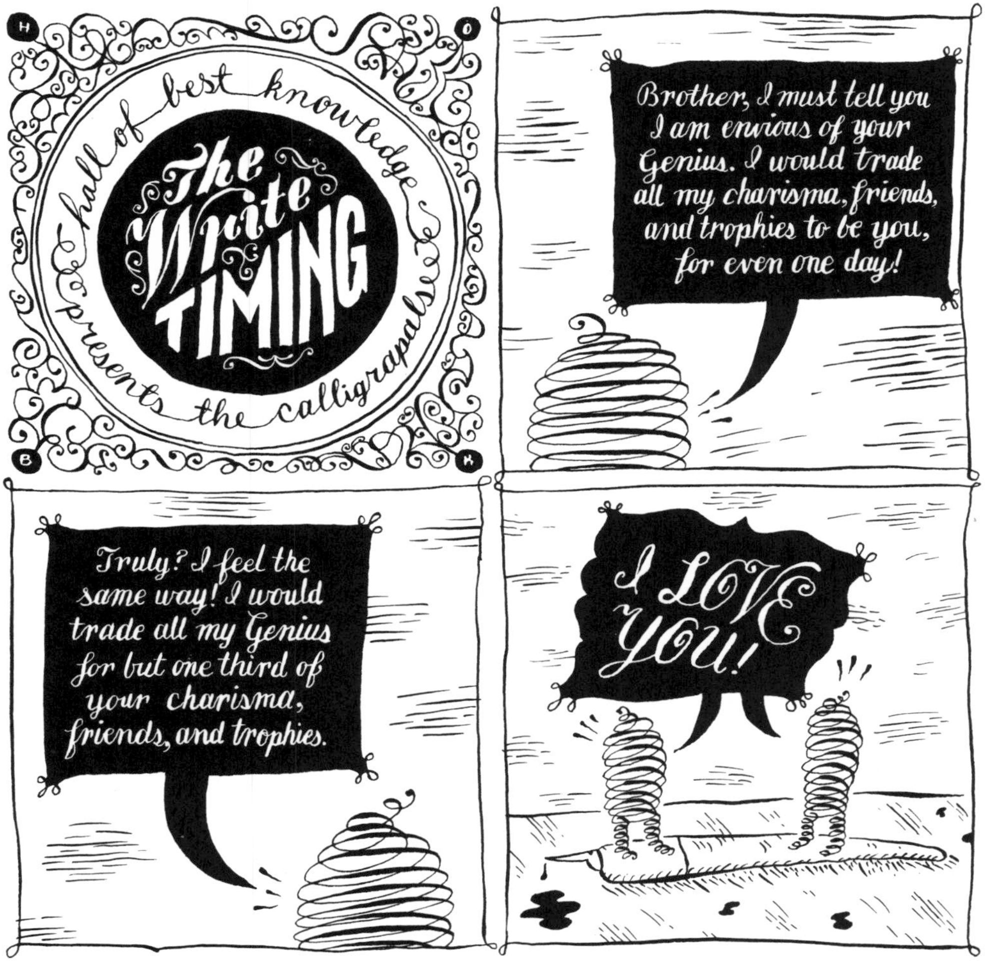
H O B K
hall of best knowledge presents the calligrapals
The Write Timing
Brother, I must tell you I am envious of your Genius. I would trade all my charisma, friends, and trophies to be you, for even one day!
Truly? I feel the same way! I would trade all my Genius for but one third of your charisma, friends, and trophies.
I LOVE YOU!

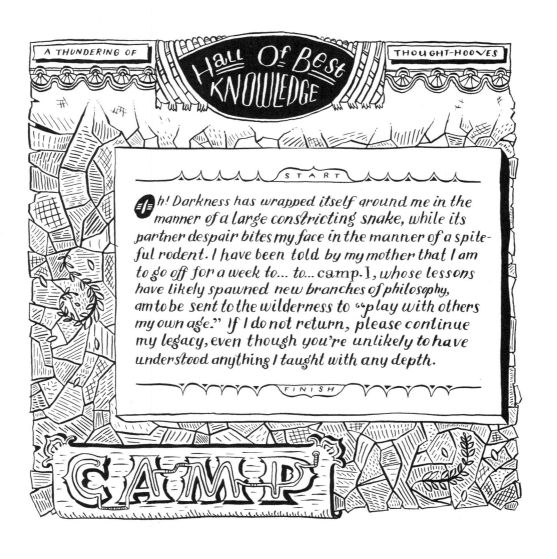

A THUNDERING OF

Hall Of Best KNOWLEDGE

THOUGHT-HOOVES

START

Oh! Darkness has wrapped itself around me in the manner of a large constricting snake, while its partner despair bites my face in the manner of a spiteful rodent. I have been told by my mother that I am to go off for a week to... to... camp. I, whose lessons have likely spawned new branches of philosophy, am to be sent to the wilderness to "play with others my own age." If I do not return, please continue my legacy, even though you're unlikely to have understood anything I taught with any depth.

FINISH

CAMP

Diarrhea-Face,

Some friends and I decided that in your absence we should break in your room and see what in gods name it is you **DO** in here all the time. I had assumed it was either crying or masturbating, or both, but no, even more depressing is this little book of yours. With these, what do you call them? Lessons? Hahaha, I mean who do you think reads these stupid things? It was funny at first — Chaz nearly shit his pants — but then once we saw how many there were... I mean it's just embarrassing. And for the record, numbnuts, you are **NOT** a genius, you're just a loser with a fancy little diary.

Hope you're being drowned at camp,

BRO

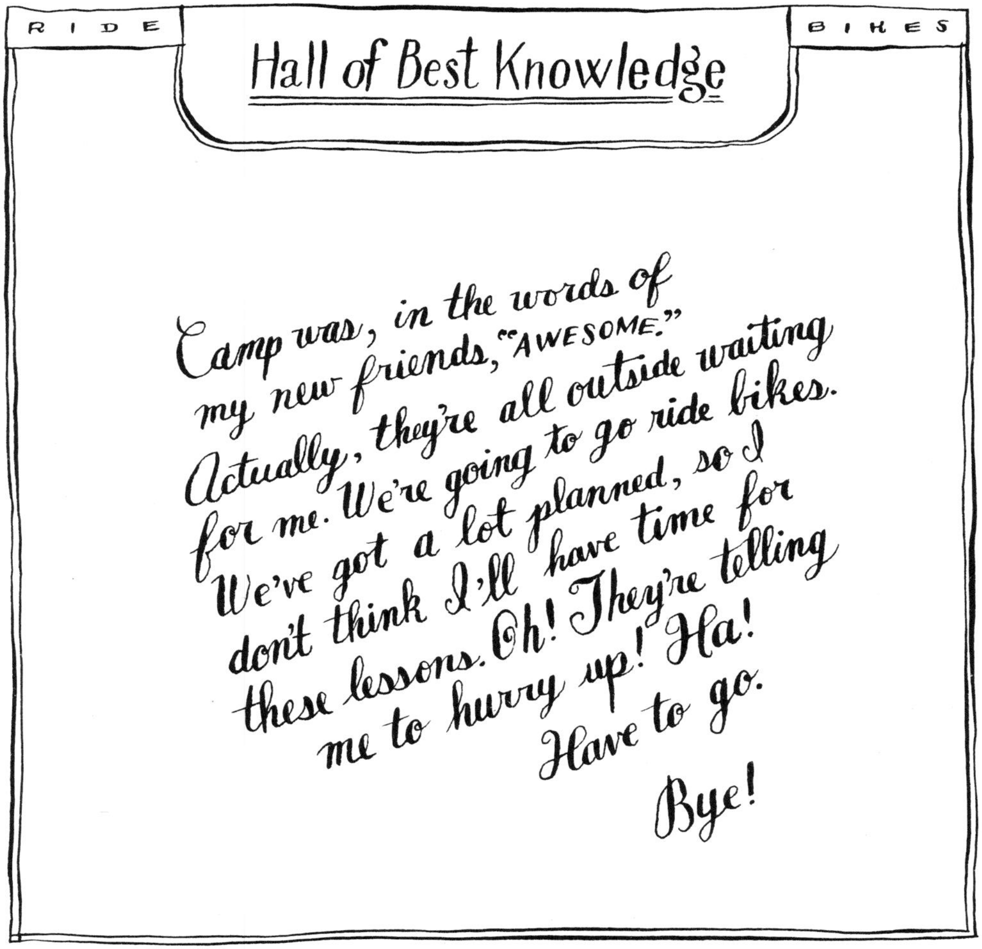
RIDE
BIKES
Hall of Best Knowledge
Camp was, in the words of my new friends, "AWESOME." Actually, they're all outside waiting for me. We're going to go ride bikes. We've got a lot planned, so I don't think I'll have time for these lessons. Oh! They're telling me to hurry up! Ha! Have to go.
Bye!